D1557839

SALVATION-HISTORY
IN THE PROLOGUE OF JOHN

SUPPLEMENTS TO

NOVUM TESTAMENTUM

EDITORIAL STAFF

C. K. BARRETT, Durham

A. F. J. KLIJN, Groningen—J. SMIT SIBINGA, Amsterdam

Editorial Secretary: H. J. DE JONGE, Leiden

VOLUME LX

SALVATION-HISTORY IN THE PROLOGUE OF JOHN

THE SIGNIFICANCE OF JOHN 1:3/4

BY

ED. L. MILLER

UNIVERSITY OF COLORADO

E.J. BRILL

LEIDEN · NEW YORK · KØBENHAVN · KÖLN

1989

Library of Congress Cataloging-in-Publication Data

Miller, Ed. L. (Eddie LeRoy), 1937-
  Salvation history in the prologue of John.
  (Supplements to Novum Testamentum, 0167-9732; v. 60)
  1. Bible. N.T. John I, 3-4—Criticism, inter-
pretation, etc. 2. History (Theology)—Biblical
teaching. 3. Salvation—Biblical teaching.
I. Title. II. Series.
BS2615.2.M526   1988   226'.506   88-24174
ISBN 90-04-08692-7

ISSN 0167-9732
ISBN 90 04 08692 7

PRINTED IN THE NETHERLANDS BY E. J. BRILL

MEIS QVATTVOR MAGISTRIS

Kenneth E. Poure
Paul J. W. Miller
Oscar Cullmann
Bo Reicke

CONTENTS

ABBREVIATIONS

BVC	Bible et Vie Chrétienne
BZ	Biblische Zeitschrift
CBQ	Catholic Biblical Quarterly
CJT	Canadian Journal of Theology
EB	Estudios Biblicos
EQ	Evangelical Quarterly
ET	Expository Times
JBL	Journal of Biblical Literature
JTS	Journal of Theological Studies
NT	Novum Testamentum
NTS	New Testament Studies
PG	Patrologia Graeca (Migne)
PL	Patrologia Latina (Migne)
RB	Revue Biblique
RHE	Revue d'Histoire Ecclésiastique
RSR	Recherches de Science Religieuse
SE	Science et Esprit
STU	Schweizerische theologische Umschau
TL	Theologische Literaturzeitung
TR	Theologische Rundschau
TWNT	Theologisches Wörterbuch zum Neuen Testament (Kittel/Friedrich)
TZ	Theologische Zeitschrift
VC	Vigiliae Christianae
VD	Verbum Domini
ZKT	Zeitschrift für Katholische Theologie
ZNW	Zeitschrift für die neutestamentliche Wissenschaft
ZTK	Zeitschrift für Theologie und Kirche

PREFACE

The present work grows out of many years of continuing interest in issues and problems in the Prologue to the Gospel of John, and it is a systematic and exhaustive treatment of one of those problems. Its appearance owes much to my study and experience at the University of Basel. I am primarily indebted to Prof. Dr. Bo Reicke for his instruction and example which have extended far beyond the academic, and I regret that his death preceded the appearance of this work in which he took much interest. I am indebted also to Prof. Dr. Jan Lochman for his attention to this study, and to Prof. Dr. Oscar Cullmann who for many years has been for me a theological inspiration and has encouraged me in the present work. Yet further I wish to thank my assistants, Mr. John S. Meyer, Mr. Damian Baumgardner, Mr. James Otte and especially Mr. Michael McCloskey for help with the preparation of the manuscript, as well as my friends Herr Heinrich Senn and Dr. Paul Keyser. My gratitude is extended to the Bibliothèque Bodmer for permission to reproduce a leaf from P[75], and to the editor of the *Theologische Zeitschrift* for permission to reproduce the substance of two of my articles. I wish to acknowledge also the Committee on University Scholarly Publications, of the University of Colorado, for a subvention award which helped make possible the publication of this volume.

I have employed my own translation in the case of the Johannine passages; elsewhere, and when not otherwise noted, I have employed the translation of the Revised Standard Version.

INTRODUCTION

In *De Civitate Dei*, St. Augustine reports, with approval, that a Platonist philosopher was once heard to say that the first five verses of John's Gospel were worthy to be written in gold and displayed in the most prominent place in every church.[1] To be sure, the entire Prologue of John (vss. 1:1-18) may be the most majestic passage in the New Testament from a purely literary standpoint, and the most exalted from a theological and philosophical standpoint. Not surprisingly, then, it is also one of the most carefully scrutinized, analyzed, and argued passages in the entire Bible, and many will be naturally skeptical that any radically new theses about the Prologue could be made good.

The fact is, however, that in more than one respect the usual approaches to the Johannine Prologue have been, probably, entirely misguided. No doubt the best example of this is the notorious effort of scholars to locate the origin of the Logos-concept which dominates the Prologue. Their attempts to trace this concept to some pre-Johannine milieu such as the *dabar* and *hochma* traditions of the Old Testament and Apocrypha, or wisdom speculations of later Jewish literature, or Greek philosophical strains, or Gnosticism, and the like, are utterly misplaced and in the end serve only to dilute and confuse the original meaning and power of John's Logos.

But one cannot do everything at once. Here we are concerned with a different issue in the Prologue, and one which, likewise, has not yet been adequately considered. The issue is, specifically, the old problem of the division and punctuation between vss. 3 and 4 of John 1. For all of its antiquity and continuing interest, neither the full resolution of the textual problem involved here nor the proper interpretation of the resulting text has heretofore been appreciated nor, therefore, the theological and literary implications of this interpretation. All of this we undertake in the present study.[2] It is at once an exegetical and theological study inasmuch as it ranges over issues from textual criticism to contemporary theological thought; it moves from the particular to the general in that our analysis centers on a single phrase from which we deduce a meaning for the whole; and it ventures from the known into the unknown in that the proper text of John 1:3/4 (that is, the division between vss. 3 and 4) is

---

[1] St. Augustine, *De Civitate Dei*, X, 29 (*PL*, 41, 307-8).

[2] The main conclusions have been anticipated in my article "The Logic of the Logos Hymn: A New View," *NTS*, 29 (1983), pp. 552ff. Some of the wording of that article is reproduced in the present work, especially in the first section of Chapter 3.

more and more recognized, whereas its implications for the first five verses, for the whole Prologue, and in fact for the whole Gospel of John, have not been.

Preliminaries on the Prologue[3]

Before we turn to a complete discussion of this problem, it will be useful to mention at least some of our convictions about the Johannine Prologue in general, though the specific question of a Logos hymn will require a somewhat more careful consideration.

---

[3] The literature on the Prologue of John is vast. At the risk of some arbitrariness we may note here in chronological order some relatively recent and general discussions which are not only important in their own right, but usually reflect earlier work and provide further bibliographical direction: M.-E. Boismard, *Le Prologue de Saint Jean* (Paris: Les Éditions du Cerf, 1953); Humphrey C. Green, "The Composition of St. John's Prologue," *ET*, 66 (1954-55), pp. 291ff.; Heinrich Schlier, "Im Anfang war das Wort: Zum Prolog des Johannesevangeliums," in *Die Zeit der Kirche: Exegetische Aufsätze und Vorträge* (Freiburg/Breisgau: Herder, 1956), pp. 274ff.; Serafín de Ausejo, "¿Es un Himno a Cristo el Prólogo de San Juan?: Los Himnos Cristologicos de la Iglesia Primitiva y el Prólogo del IV Evangelio," *EB*, 15 (1956), pp. 223ff., 381ff.; C. H. Dodd, "The Prologue to the Fourth Gospel and Christian Worship," in *Studies in the Fourth Gospel*, ed. F. L. Cross (London: Mowbray, 1957), pp. 9ff.; Ernst Käsemann, "Aufbau und Anliegen des johanneischen Prologs," in *Libertas Christiana* (Munich: Kaiser, 1957), pp. 75ff.; M.-F. Lacan, "L'Oeuvre du Verbe Incarné: Le Don de la Vie (Jo.1:4)," *RSR*, 45 (1957), pp. 61ff.; Rudolf Schnackenburg, "Logos-Hymnus und johanneischer Prolog," *BZ*, 1 (1957), pp. 69ff.; Siegfried Schulz, *Komposition und Herkunft der johanneischen Reden* (Stuttgart: Kohlhammer, 1960), pp. 7ff.; J. A. T. Robinson, "The Relation of the Prologue to the Gospel of St. John," *NTS*, 9 (1962-63), pp. 120ff.; Ernst Haenchen, "Probleme des johanneischen 'Prologs,'" *ZTK*, 60 (1963), pp. 305ff.; Walther Eltester, "Der Logos und sein Prophet: Fragen zur heutigen Erklärung des johanneischen Prologs," in *Apophoreta* (Berlin: Töpelmann, 1964), pp. 109ff.; P. Lamarche, "Le Prologue de Jean," *RSR*, 52 (1964), pp. 497ff.; Joachim Jeremias, "The Revealing Word," in *The Central Message of the New Testament* (Philadelphia: Fortress Press, 1965), pp. 71ff.; Rudolf Schnackenburg, *Das Johannesevangelium* (Freiburg/Breisgau: Herder, 1965-75), I, pp. 197ff.; Raymond E. Brown, *The Gospel according to John: I-XIII* (Garden City, N.Y.: Doubleday, 1966-70), I, pp. 1ff.; Henri van den Bussche, "De tout Être la Parole était la Vie: Jean 1:1-5," *BVC*, 69 (1966), pp. 57ff.; Hermann Ridderbos, "The Structure and Scope of the Prologue to the Gospel of John," *NT*, 8 (1966), pp. 180ff.; Christoph Demke, "Der sogennante Logos-Hymnus im johanneischen Prolog," *ZNW*, 58 (1967), pp. 45ff.; A. Feuillet, *Le Prologue du Quatrième Évangile: Étude de Théologie Johannique* (Paris: Desclée de Brouwer, 1968); J. C. O'Neill, "The Prologue to St. John's Gospel," *JTS*, 20 (1969), pp. 41ff.; Peder Borgen, "Observations on the Targumic Character of the Prologue of John," *NTS*, 16 (1970), pp. 288ff.; Morna Hooker, "John the Baptist and the Johannine Prologue," *NTS*, 16 (1970), 354ff.; Robert Kysar, "The Background of the Prologue of the Fourth Gospel: A Critique of Historical Methods," *CJT*, 16 (1970) pp. 250ff.; Jean Irigoin, "La Composition rythmique du Prologue de Jean (1:1-18)," *RB*, 78 (1971), pp. 501ff.; Jack T. Sanders, *The New Testament Christological Hymns: Their Historical Religious Background* (Cambridge, England: Cambridge University Press, 1971), pp. 20ff. and Ch. 2; Dosithée Atal, *Structure et Signification des Cinq Premiers Versets de L'Hymne Johannique au Logos* (Louvain: Nauwelaerts, 1972); C. K. Barrett, "The Prologue of St. John's Gospel," in *New Testament Essays* (London: SPCK, 1972), pp. 27ff.; Peder Borgen, "Logos was the True Light: Contributions to the Interpretation of

We state, then, simply and without argument our view that (1) the Prologue (John 1:1-18) is a literary and theological unity and, notwithstanding its obvious connection with the Fourth Gospel "proper" (John 1:19-20:30), must be viewed as a separate composition; (2) the Gospel proper was written first, followed by the First Epistle, and finally the Prologue;[4] (3) in their original forms these derived certainly from the same theological circle and, in fact, were probably composed by the same

---

the Prologue of John," *NT*, 14 (1972), pp. 115ff.; R. G. Hamerton-Kelly, *Pre-Existence, Wisdom, and the Son of Man: A Study of the Idea of Pre-Existence in the New Testament* (Cambridge, England: Cambridge University Press, 1973), pp. 200ff.; Edwin D. Freed, "Some Old Testament Influences on the Prologue of John," in *A Light unto My Path: Old Testament Studies in Honor of Jacob M. Myers*, ed. Howard N. Bream, Ralph D. Heim, Carey A. Moore (Philadelphia: Temple University Press, 1974), pp. 145ff.; J. S. King, "The Prologue to the Fourth Gospel: Some Unsolved Problems," *ET*, 86 (1974), pp. 372ff.; Howard M. Teeple, *The Literary Origin of the Gospel of John* (Evanston, Ill.: Religion and Ethics Institute, 1974), pp. 126ff.; Heinrich Zimmermann, "Christushymnus und johanneischer Prolog," in *Neues Testament und Kirche*, ed. Joachim Gnilka (Freiburg/Breisgau: Herder, 1974), pp. 249ff.; Eldon Jay Epp, "Wisdom, Torah, Word: The Johannine Prologue and the Purpose of the Fourth Gospel," in *Current Issues in Biblical and Patristic Interpretation*, ed. Gerald F. Hawthorne (Grand Rapids, Mich.: Eerdmans, 1975), pp. 128ff.; Morna Hooker, "The Johannine Prologue and the Messianic Secret," *NTS*, 21 (1975), pp. 40ff.; Mathias Rissi, "Die Logoslieder im Prolog des vierten Evangeliums," *TZ*, 31 (1975), pp. 321ff.; Hartmut Gese, "Der Johannesprolog," in *Zur biblischen Theologie: Altestamentliche Vorträge* (Munich: Kaiser, 1977), pp. 152ff.; R. Alan Culpepper, "The Pivot of John's Prologue," *NTS*, 27 (1979), pp. 1ff.; Peter Hofrichter, "'Egeneto anthropos': Text und Zusätze im Johannesprolog," *ZNW*, 70 (1979), pp. 214ff.; Yu Ibuki, "Offene Fragen zur Aufnahme des Logoshymnus in das vierte Evangelium," *Annual of the Japanese Biblical Institute*, 5 (1979), pp. 105ff.; Juan Mateos and Juan Barreto, *El Evangelio de Juan: Analisis Linguistico y Commentario Exegetico* (Madrid: Ediciones Cristianidad, 1979), pp. 37ff.; Walter Schmithals, "Der Prolog des Johannesevangeliums," *ZNW*, 70 (1979), pp. 16ff.; Ernst Haenchen, *Das Johannesevangelium*, ed. Ulrich Busse (Tübingen: Mohr, 1980), pp. 110ff.; Michael Theobald, *Im Anfang war das Wort: Textlinguistische Studie zum Johannesprolog* (Stuttgart: Katholisches Bibelwerk, 1983); Ignace de la Potterie, "Structure du Prologue de Saint Jean," *NTS*, 30 (1984), pp. 354ff.; John Painter, "Christology and the History of the Johannine Community in the Prologue of the Fourth Gospel," *NTS*, 30 (1984), pp. 460ff.; Eugen Ruckstuhl, "Kritische Arbeit am Johannesprolog," in *The New Testament Age*, ed. William C. Weinrich (Atlanta: Mercer University Press, 1984), II, pp. 443ff.; Charles Homer Giblin, "Two Complementary Literary Structures in John 1:1-18," *JBL*, 104 (1985), pp. 87ff.; Gérard Rochais, "La Formation du Prologue (Jn. 1:1-18)," *SE*, 37 (1985), pp. 5ff., 161ff. Special note should be made of the bibliography on the Prologue in E. Malatesta, *St. John's Gospel 1920-1965: A Cumulative and Classified Bibliography of Books and Periodical Literature on the Fourth Gospel* (Rome: Pontifical Biblical Institute, 1967), pp. 69ff., and, subsequently, Hartwig Thyen's discussion, "Aufweis der Forschungstrends an neuern Interpretationsversuchen des Johannesprologs," in his "Aus der Literatur zum Johannesevangelium," *TR*, 39 (1975), pp. 53ff. Still more recent, and otherwise excellent, are the bibliographies printed in the English edition of Haenchen's commentary: *A Commentary on the Gospel of John*, ed. Ulrich Busse, tr. and ed. Robert W. Funk (Philadelphia: Fortress Press, 1984), I, pp. 103ff., 131ff.

    [4] We leave out of account the chronological placing of II and III John and of John 21. These do not bear on the present issues.

individual;[5] (4) though composed separately from the Fourth Gospel proper, the Prologue stands in an essential relationship to it, both from a literary and theological standpoint;[6] (5) it stands in an even closer relationship to I John 1:1-4 which probably served in some ways as a model or draft for parts of the Prologue;[7] (6) notwithstanding its broad literary and theological unity (the first point above), upon closer examination the Prologue is actually a mosaic or anthology consisting of hymnic material, narrative material, miscellaneous lines, and later interpolations; (7) the *Urstoff* or foundation-piece of the Prologue material is a Logos hymn in vss. 1:1a-b, 3-5, to which yet other short Johannine pieces and quotations (vss. 9-14, 16-18) were added, attached like barnacles on a ship's hull;[8] (8) the whole of this material was eventually attached to the Fourth Gospel proper, and in time a sort of "splicing" occurred when the original opening of the Gospel appeared as vss. 1:6-8 and an overlapping with the Gospel occurred in vs. 15 (cf. 1:30); (9) at some point interpolations made their way into the Prologue, as at vss. 1c and 2.[9]

---

[5] This, in contrast to theories about the nature and origin of the Prologue marked by complexity and flamboyance. The rise and fall of one such theory is notorious: Bultmann's thesis that the Prologue is a Christian reworking of an Aramaic and Gnostic-imbued hymn to the Baptist (advanced first in his influential 1923 essay, "Der religions-geschichtliche Hintergrund des Prologs zum Johannesevangelium," in *EYX-APIΣTHPION: Studien zur Religion und Literatur des Alten und Neuen Testaments*, ed. Hans Schmidt (Göttingen: Vandenhoeck & Ruprecht, 1923), II, pp. 3ff., and maintained later in his commentary on John (*Das Evangelium des Johannes* (Göttingen: Vandenhoeck & Ruprecht, 1941), pp. 3ff.) proved for a time to be very influencial but is now dead. Cf. the comment of Käsemann, Bultmann's own student: "Der vorchristliche Charakter des Hymnus ist mehr als problematisch, das aramäische Original unglaubwürdig, das angenommene Täuferlied eine reine Hypothese" ("Aufbau und Anliegen des johanneischen Prologs," p. 86).

[6] Generally, we resist certain recent proposals to dissect and dissolve the Fourth Gospel into sources, strata, redactions, dislocations, and influences, as being largely speculative, often radically divergent from one another, and introducing unnecessary complications. We agree with Oscar Cullmann that in regard to such proposals what is called for is restraint (cf. *Der johanneische Kreis: Sein Platz im Spätjudentum, in der Jüngerschaft Jesu und im Urchristentum* (Tübingen: Mohr, 1975), Ch. 1, *passim*). In any event, it appears that the dissecting and dissolving onslaught has not (at least not yet) carried the day against those who have argued persuasively for the fundamental unity of the Johannine Gospel, most notably Eugen Ruckstuhl in *Die literarische Einheit des Johannesevangeliums: Gegenwärtige Stand der einschlägigen Forschungen* (Freiburg/Schweiz: Paulus, 1951).

[7] Our general view of the Prologue as composed separately from the Gospel proper and yet as being one with it both literarily and theologically, and as partly modelled after I John 1:1-4, has much in common with the view expressed by J. A. T. Robinson, "The Relation of the Prologue to the Gospel of St. John," pp. 120ff.

[8] This is to be distinguished from the hypothesis of an *Urprolog* to which or into which editorial comments have been attached or inserted.

[9] With respect to the development of the Fourth Gospel as a whole, in contrast to highly convoluted theories we are tempted by a simple four-stage development: (1) The Beloved Disciple (not John the Son of Zebedee) passed on to his disciples his eyewitness accounts of Jesus; (2) one of his disciples incorporated these traditions in his composition of the

The specific question of a Logos hymn in the Prologue is more critical for our present study.[10] Certainly the Prologue is "poetic," both in a loose and strict sense. Because of its cadences, majestic language, and lofty concepts, the Prologue of John is rightly considered one of the most exalted passages in the Bible, "worthy to be written in gold." On the other hand, within the Prologue itself some lines bear the marks of even more deliberate and careful design.[11] In viewing these lines as poetic in the stricter sense, we do not mean that they are structured by stress or quantity but that they are artfully composed in the Semitic style of parallelisms. We believe, in fact, that these lines involve a complete Christological hymn of much the same sort as found elsewhere in the New Testament,[12] and, possibly, fragments of yet other hymns.

We have already suggested that the Prologue is an anthology of short Johannine pieces, and, if correct, this immediately precludes not only that the Prologue was composed as a complete piece just as we have it,[13] but also the discovery there of any pervasive structure, whether it be, for example, an elaborate chiasm[14] or extended Targumic exposition.[15] That

original Gospel, the Fourth Gospel "proper," (3) after the death of the Beloved Disciple, this same author issued an expanded version, now including Ch. 21, (4) to this second edition the Prologue material was eventually attached, and some minor interpolations were introduced throughout the Gospel.

[10] On New Testament and early Christian hymns (and relevant literature), see Gottfried Schille, *Frühchristliche Hymnen* (Berlin: Evangelische Verlagsanstalt, 1962); Reinhard Deichgräber, *Gotteshymnus und Christushymnus in der frühen Christenheit: Untersuchungen zu Form, Sprache und Stil der frühchristlichen Hymnen* (Göttingen: Vandenhoeck & Ruprect, 1967). Schille treats the Prologue as containing an epiphany hymn (pp. 121ff.); Deichgräber treats it not at all: "Eigentlich müsste bei den Christushymnen auch J 1, 1ff. behandelt werden. Doch würde dieser Text wegen seiner besonderen Problematik eine spezielle Untersuchung verlangen, die den Rahmen dieser Untersuchung sprengen würde, weswegen wir ihn hier ausgeklammert haben" (p. 118, n. 3). On the hymnic character of the Prologue, see the relevant citations in note 3 above; indeed, many of the works cited there deal also with this topic.

[11] Nearly all Johannine scholars would agree with this much. Jeremias extended the claim to cover the whole Prologue: "The Prologue, as everyone knows today, is a powerfully contrived song, an early Christian religious poem, a psalm, a hymn to the Logos Jesus Christ" ("The Revealing Word," p. 72). One of the few who find no special poetry whatsoever in the Prologue is Barrett ("The Prologue of St. John's Gospel," pp. 36ff.).

[12] The hymnic material in the Prologue has most in common with Phil. 2:6-11 and Col. 1:15-20. On the (logical) relation of these and other passages to the Prologue hymn, see the brief discussion by Brown, *The Gospel according to John*, I, pp. 20f., and his comment on the possible relevance of the *Odes of Solomon*. For a more exhaustive treatment of the possible relationships of the Prologue to its religious and literary environment, see Jack T. Sanders, *The New Testament Christological Hymns*, pp. 20ff. and Ch. 2, though this work labors too much under the spell of the *religionsgeschichtliche Schule* and, like much New Testament scholarship, tends to be swept away with its own complexity.

[13] For Example, Barrett, "The Prologue of St. John's Gospel," and Ruckstuhl, *Die literarische Einheit des Johannesevangeliums*, pp. 63ff.

[14] As in Culpepper, "The Pivot of John's Prologue."

[15] As in Borgen, "Observations on the Targumic Character of the Prologue of John."

the Prologue as a whole cannot be equated with a Johannine hymn (or, for that matter, any extended structure) is *prima facie* apparent from the frequently noted "joints and seams," the intrusion of narrative material at vss. 6-8,[16] and the overlapping of vs. 15 with 1:30. Even so, many asymmetries yet persist in the remaining lines: overlapping references to the incarnation at vss. 9,[17] 10, and 14 (and, we will argue later, at vs. 4a), the switch from the third to the first person at vs. 14, and irregular rhythms and groupings of lines at vss. 8-14, 16-18. Thus even the possibility of identifying a hymn *strewn throughout* the Prologue is immediately thrown into doubt. And the doubt is augmented by the divergence of opinion on the whereabouts of such a hymn (aside from disagreements about strophes and the ordering of lines) as in the following comparisons:[18]

Burney	vss. 1-5	10b-11	14abe	16a, 17	
Bernard	1-5	10-11	14		18
Gächter	1-5	10-12	14	16-17	
Bultmann	1-5	10bc-12b	14	16	
De Ausejo	1-5	9-11	14	16	18
Schlier	1-5	9-12b	14	16	
Käsemann	1, 3-5	10-12			
Schnackenburg	1, 3-4	9ab, 10ac-11	14abe	16	
Schille	1, 3-5	10-11a	14	16-17	
Haenchen	1-5	9-11	14	16-17	
Brown	1-5	10-12b	14	16	
Feuillet	1-5	9-12b	14	16-18	
O'Neill	1-5	10-12c, 13abd	14b-e	16a	18
Sanders	1-5	9-11			
Rissi	1-5	10ac, 11-12b	14, 15c	16-17	
Schmithals	1-5	12ab	14	17	
Rochais	1, 3-5	10-12b	14	16	

---

[16] Thus most scholars. I am entirely unconvinced by Barrett's argument for the continuity of these lines with the rest of the Prologue ("The Prologue of St. John's Gospel," pp. 39ff.). Rather, the continuity of vss. 6-8 with vss. 19ff. is unmistakable.

[17] A good case can be made for taking ἐρχόμενον εἰς τὸν κόσμον as modifying τὸ φῶς τὸ ἀληθινόν on the basis of the immediate context (cf. vs. 10) and Johannine usage throughout the Gospel (as in 3:19 and 12:46). See below, p. 84, n. 118.

[18] Charles Fox Burney, *The Aramaic Origin of the Fourth Gospel* (Oxford, England: Oxford University Press, 1922), pp. 41f.; J. H. Bernard, *A Critical and Exegetical Commentary on the Gospel according to St. John*, ed. A. H. McNeile (Edinburgh: Clark, 1928), I, pp. cxliv ff.; Paul Gächter, "Strophe im Johannesevangelium," *ZKT*, 60 (1936), pp. 99ff.; Bultmann, *Das Evangelium des Johannes*, pp. 1ff.; de Ausejo, "¿Es un Himno a Cristo el Prólogo de San Juan?" pp. 392ff.; Schlier, "Im Anfang war das Wort," pp. 274ff.; Haenchen, "Probleme des johanneischen 'Prologs'," pp. 305ff.; Käsemann, "Aufbau und Anliegen des johanneischen Prologs," pp. 75ff.; Schnackenburg, *Das Johannesevangelium*, I, pp. 200ff., and his earlier "Logos-Hymnus und johanneischer Prolog," *BZ*, I (1957), pp. 69ff.; Schille, *Frühchristliche Hymnen*, pp. 122ff.; Brown, *The Gospel according to John*, I,

We are not nearly so optimistic as these scholars. Even on the hypothesis (which we do not share) of a hymn strewn throughout the Prologue, it is clearly impossible to reconstruct it with any confidence, to say nothing of the fact that this impossibility renders the hypothesis itself nearly meaningless.[19]

If, however, we focus our attention on vss. 1-5 only, a quite different impression emerges. As Atal expresses it,

> Dès l'abord, les cinq premiers versets du Prologue frappent par leur unité. Celle-ci apparaît complète, ininterrompue et fortement marquée par un style uniforme.[20]

Most Prologue scholars accept vss. 1:1-5 as containing hymnic material and they are certainly correct in this. The hymnic character of vss. 1:1-5 is suggested in fact by six converging lines of evidence. While no one of these in itself may be decisive, all of them taken together constitute an impressive exhibit.

(i) The exalted ideas and panoramic vision of these verses, enhanced with the metaphor/title Logos, is acknowledged by all. This poetic tone immediately calls attention to itself and not only distinguishes these verses from the remainder of the Prologue and the Gospel but enrolls them with the loftiest passages in the entire Bible.

(ii) Closely related, we have here a third-person Christological concentration in which the Logos is glorified and his deeds narrated.

(iii) More specifically, the passage involves the unmistakable imprint of the most notable device of Hebrew poetry. In vss. 1a-b, 3-5 we have a series of four clearly conceived *parallelismi membrorum*: Vs. 1a-b is a climactic parallelism,

---

pp. 21ff.; Feuillet, *Le Prologue du Quatrième Évangile*, pp. 196ff.; J. C. O'Neill, "The Prologue to St. John's Gospel," pp. 45ff.; J. T. Sanders, *The New Testament Christological Hymns*, pp. 20ff.; Rissi, "Die Logoslieder im Prolog des vierten Evangeliums," pp. 321ff; Schmithals, "Der Prolog des Johannnesevangeliums," pp. 16ff.; Rochais, "La Formation du Prologue (Jn. 1:1-18)," pp. 5ff. For a still longer list, see Rochais, "La Formation du Prologue (Jn. 1:1-18)," pp. 7ff. A useful discussion entitled "Landmarks in Prologue Reconstruction" may be found in Teeple, *The Literary Origin of the Fourth Gospel*, pp. 126ff., though Teeple's own proposal (pp. 132ff.) is an example of a much too speculative and heavy-handed reconstruction.

[19] Writing in 1964, Walther Eltester surveyed the major contributions to the study of the Logos Hymn and concluded that "die Differenzen über den Umfang dieses Hymnus, über seinen Aufbau, seine rhythmische Form, schliesslich doch auch immer noch über seine konkrete Herkunft sind doch so gross, dass man mit Käsemann feststellen muss: 'Erfreulich ist dieser Diskussionsstand nicht' " ("Der Logos und sein Prophet," pp. 115f.). Over twenty years later the "Diskussionsstand" is no more encouraging.

[20] Atal, *Structure et Signification des Cinq Premiers Versets de L'Hymne Johannique au Logos*, p. 19.

In the beginning was the Logos,
And the Logos was with God.

Vs. 3 is an antithetical parallelism,

All things came into being through him,
And apart from him nothing came into being.[21]

Vs. 4 is a climactic parallelism,

What has appeared in him was Life,
And the Life was the Light of men.

And vs. 5 is both a climactic and antithetical parallelism,

And the Light shines in the Darkness,
And the Darkness cannot overcome it.[22]

These parallelisms bear every mark of being deliberately composed for the occasion, and they are the only instances of an intensified and extended use of this literary device in the Prologue. Their conspicuous presence in vss. 1-5 immediately casts a certain poetic light on these verses.

(iv) Also conspicuous by its presence in vss. 1-5, and also reflecting a Hebrew poetic motif, is the "staircase" structure which dominates vss. 1a-b, 4, and 5, where the last element of a clause becomes the first element of the subsequent clause: $A \rightarrow B$, $B \rightarrow C$, $C \rightarrow D$. It is to be noted that we are dealing here with a wider structuring principle than parallelism inasmuch as this principle, at least in the case of vss. 4-5, structures parallelisms themselves. Again, this device is not employed in so polished and extended a manner elsewhere in the Prologue. Admittedly, it is not sustained even throughout vss. 1-5; but where it does occur, in vs. 1a-b and vss. 4-5, it can hardly be accidental, and again, it imparts an unmistakable poetic flavor to the whole of these verses.[23]

---

[21] Here and in the following parallelism we are taking ὃ γέγονεν with vs. 4. That this is the correct reading is one of the major theses of the present study, but the present claim about parallelisms is not dependent on it.

[22] There is no satisfactory way in English to reproduce the double meaning—except perhaps "master"—of καταλαμβάνω, which means both to overpower and to understand. Cf. Brown's brief discussion of four tendencies in the interpretation of κατέλαβεν (*The Gospel according to John*, I, p. 8). That John actually intended "overcome" seems clear from his usage of καταλαμβάνω at 12:35. On our attempt to reproduce the gnomic aorist with "cannot overcome it," see below p. 94.

[23] With respect to parallelism and stair-case structuring, see Brown's discussion on "the poetic format of the Gospel discourses" (*The Gospel according to John*, I, pp. cxxxii ff.). Brown documents instances of these devices as employed throughout the Gospel but rightfully contrasts the "quasi-poetic" character of the discourses with the "far more carefully worked out poetic style" of the Prologue (p. cxxxiii). We, of course, are arguing that in the first five verses we have a still more sustained employment of these devices than even

(v) By contrast with the rest of the Prologue, in vss. 1-5 we have a sequence of many lines of the same relative length resulting in a sustained poetic rhythm.

Arguments for the poetic nature of John 1:1-5 usually include, rightfully, such observations as the above. These considerations may in fact suffice for the argument, especially in view of the "dissonances" which exist by contrast in the verses immediately following: We have already mentioned the intrusion of narrative material, the several overlapping references to the incarnation, the switch from the third-person to the first-person, and the irregularities in both rhythm and in the groupings of the lines.[24] We believe, however, that the case for the poetic character of John 1:1-5 can be made yet stronger.

(vi) If vss. 1c and 2 are deleted, not only is the poetic character of the remaining lines thereby greatly enhanced but they take on the appearance of a *block* of lines, unified and self-contained. For the result is a series of lines of the same relative length[25] and which, furthermore, fall into a series of four couplets, each with its own distinct point sustained over two lines, but at the same time supplementing or advancing the previous points—something unparalleled in the rest of the Prologue. But of course it must be asked: On what possible grounds might vss. 1c and 2 be thrown into doubt and excluded? It is important to note that in speculating on the secondary character of these two lines we are no more extravagant than other interpreters who seek variously to distinguish the original hymnic material in the Prologue from the Evangelist's or redactors' interpolations, and especially those who do so precisely at vs. 2![26]

To start with, it is at least relevant that these lines do not so neatly form a parallelism such as we find with all of the others in vss. 1-5. Vs. 1c, "and

in the remainder of the Prologue. Cf. Atal's treatment of the parallelisms and "mots-agrafe" (*Structure et Signification des Cinq Premiers Versets de L'Hymne Johannique au Logos*, pp. 22ff.) and his summary comment: "Cet état de choses où apparaît le caractère répétitoire des versets en même temps que le développement des idées en spirale, explique la merveilleuse originalité littéraire des vv. 1-5 du Prologue" (p. 27).

[24] It may be countered that the remainder of the Prologue (excluding the narrative verses, 6-8, 15) is not as "dissonant" as we have suggested, for one finds there further instances of parallelism, rhythmic lines, couplets, and the like. But nowhere are there the sustained examples of these that we find in vss. 1- 5. And, in any event, we are not denying that there is no hymnic material beyond vss. 1-5. We ourselves have suggested already that beyond vss. 1-5 the Prologue is a collection of various Johannine pieces. Why should not at least some of this material bear a poetic stamp or even be short quotations from other hymns?

[25] Again, for the moment taking ὃ γέγονεν as beginning vs. 4.

[26] Cf. the chart above, and O'Neill's observations on interpolations in the Prologue ("The Prologue to St. John's Gospel," pp. 41ff.).

the Logos was God," obviously continues and qualifies the statement immediately preceding it in vs. 1b, "and the Word was with God," whereas vs. 2, "This one was in the beginning with God," clearly harks back to the first two lines vs. 1, "In the beginning was the Word, and the Word was with God." Thus the two lines of vss. 1c and 2 look in two entirely different directions and, by contrast with *all* the other lines in 1:1-5 which form parallelisms, create a jarring dissonance from a stylistic and literary standpoint. Closely related is the observation that only superficially does the staircase pattern extend from vs. 1:1a-b into vs. 1:1c. It is true that vs. 1:1c begins with θεὸς, the last word of the previous line, but unlike every other instance of this device in vss. 1:1-5 it is not the subject of the sentence but rather the predicate—a conspicuous irregularity in an otherwise consistent pattern. But yet a second consideration bears on the elimination of these lines: They might easily be understood as later polemical glosses, of much the same character as many think occur elsewhere in the Gospel and even in the Prologue. Vs. 1c, which asserts the Logos' unity with God, could easily be viewed as a corrective to a possibly false impression arising from vs. 1b, which, at least implicitly, asserts his distinction from God; if so, the two lines could be interpreted with the emphasis, "and the Logos was with God (and make no mistake, the Logos *was* God)." Likewise, in vs. 2 we might have an attempt to correct a possible misunderstanding arising from vs. 1a-b; it is not the case that the Logos "was in the beginning" and at a later time "was with God," but rather the Logos "was in the beginning with God".[27] Both of these considerations, when taken together, cast a strong doubt on the original unity of vss. 1c and 2 with the rest of the material in the first verses of John.

The case is aesthetic and conjectural. We may not, therefore, insist on the deletion of these lines, but neither is their deletion crucial. Even if they are retained as lines of the hymn their presence would in no way affect the theological interpretation which will be proposed for the passage. Nonetheless, we ourselves find the case for the deletion of vss. 1c-2 persuasive. The result is, in the way already suggested, a still firmer case for a Logos hymn in John 1:1-5.

---

[27] It is this very sort of reasoning that Brown employs in attributing John 4:2 to a subsequent hand: "This is clearly an attempt to modify iii.22, where it is said that Jesus did baptize, and serves as an almost indisputable evidence of the presence of several hands in the composition of John. Perhaps the final redactor was afraid that the sectarians of John the Baptist would use Jesus' baptizing as an argument that he was only an imitator of John the Baptist" (*The Gospel according to John*, I, p. 164).

The Thesis: Heilsgeschichte in Hymnenform

But there is more. For we have now to develop what we believe to be conclusive evidence that John 1:1a-b, 3-5 is a whole Christological hymn, complete and intact. The evidence lies in the salvation-historical structure of these verses.

We will attempt, primarily, to demonstrate the presence of a salvation-historical perspective in these verses and, secondarily, that this decisively enhances the claim about a complete Christological (indeed, salvation-historical) hymn there: *Heilsgeschichte in Hymnenform.* It should be noted that the two points are not dependent on one another: Even if the implications for the hymn should be rejected, our thesis about the salvation-historical interpretation of the passage may stand on its own. This has brought us, then, to the twofold thesis of the present study. It has also brought us to the problem.

Depending on how one understands the expression "salvation-history," it may or may not be difficult to argue for a salvation-historical perspective in the Prologue. Taking the expression in a rather loose sense, as an emphasis on the historical character of God's saving activity, almost everyone acknowledges the salvation-historical character of the Prologue. Who would deny that the advent of the pre-existent and divine Logos into the world at a certain moment in our history is indeed the focus of the Prologue? Aside from numerous supporting data throughout, surely the theological and aesthetic high point of the Prologue as a whole is the stupefying announcement in vs. 14: "And the Word became flesh and lived among us, and we beheld his glory. . . ." Surely this is, at least in a loose sense, salvation-history. If, however, salvation-history is conceived more narrowly and strictly, such that in the Prologue of John the incarnation of the Logos is seen as standing in a certain relation to other events[28] which together constitute a redemptive history, then the consensus would no doubt give way to skepticism. Nonetheless, the presence in the Prologue of salvation-history even in this narrower sense would become evident if a second claim can be argued successfully.

The second claim, which is a much more controversial one, asserts that the advent of the Logos into human history is introduced already in vs. 4 of the Prologue. This view, barely noted among the commentators, has not enjoyed a full and systematic defense, and in no case have its full implications been appreciated. We shall argue for the "incarnational" interpretation of vs. 4a, and that this suggests immediately a view of vss.

---

[28] I recognize that from a philosophical standpoint "event" may be a problematic word here, but we let it stand for the moment.

1-5 as involving a succession, continuity, and progression of saving events[29]—*Heilsgeschichte* in the narrow sense. The incarnational inter-pretation of John 1:4a and the salvation-historical interpretation of vss. 1-5 presuppose, however, a certain resolution of the problem of the punc-tuation which divides vss. 3 and 4, a resolution requiring a considerable investment of textual-critical, analytical, and theological attention. The punctuation connecting vss. 3 and 4 and the interpretation of the resulting first clause of vs. 4 will, in fact, prove to be the key which unlocks the structure and meaning of vss. 1-5. This in turn will illumine the whole Prologue, and (unless, *per impossibile*, one denies a literary and theological relation of the Prologue to the rest of the Fourth Gospel) the Fourth Gospel in general.

John 1:3/4: Reading I *and* Reading II

There are, it turns out, two different ways in which John 1:3/4 has been punctuated, resulting in two radically different readings and many com-peting interpretations. This is a very old problem, occupying the atten-tion of Biblical scholars from the early Fathers to the present. As for those who will smile skeptically at the prospect of treating a mere dot (to pass over Jesus' own insistence on the importance of small matters in Matt. 5:18), it is impossible to improve on Kurt Aland's challenge with which he introduces his own exposition, "Eine Untersuchung zu Joh. 1:3-4: Über die Bedeutung eines Punktes":

> Einen Punkt zum Gegenstand einer besonderen Untersuchung zu machen, heisst also doch wohl, eine der kleinsten Kleinigkeiten im Neuen Testament zu betrachten. Wenn sich hier Sinn, ja Notwendigkeit einer solchen Arbeit erweist, sollte Hoffnung darauf bestehen, dass das Lächeln der Exegeten über die "Kleinigkeiten," denen die Arbeit der Textkritik oft gilt, einer Ein-sicht in die Notwendigkeit der Beachtung auch der Details der Überlieferung des neutestamentlichen Textes weicht.[30]

That Aland succeeds in proving his point can hardly be denied, and his discussion is mandatory for those who desire an exhaustive survey of the

---

[29] This language is, of course, borrowed from Oscar Cullmann who takes succession, continuity, and progression to be hallmarks of the events constituting *Heilsgeschichte* or "salvation-history" in the strict sense (see especially his *Heil als Geschichte: Heilsgeschichtliche Existenz im Neuen Testament*, (Tübingen: Mohr, 1965), *passim*). We will return in our last chapter to a discussion of the theology of salvation-history.

[30] Kurt Aland, "Eine Untersuchung zu Joh. 1:3-4: Über die Bedeutung eines Punktes," *ZNW*, 59 (1968), p. 174. An abbreviated version of this study appeared in *Studies in the History and Text of the New Testament*, ed. Boyd L. Daniels and M. Jack Suggs (Salt Lake City: University of Utah Press, 1967), pp. 161ff., and the whole has been reproduced, with minor changes, in Aland's *Neutestamentliche Entwürfe* (Munich: Kaiser, 1979), pp. 351ff.

main approaches that have over the years been taken toward this text, to say nothing of the original insights contributed by Aland himself.[31] That Aland has had the last word on the dot is not, however, conceded. Though it would certainly be difficult to improve on his textual-critical treatment of the text, there yet remains the exegetical and theological problem, the problem of the interpretation of the text. On this latter question, Aland himself offers a few suggestions, but regards his work, here and in general, as a textual-critical preparation of the material with which the commentators erect their buildings.[32]

But what, then, is the problem in John 1:3/4? The passage reads as follows in its unpunctuated form:

(3) πάντα δι' αὐτοῦ ἐγένετο καὶ χωρὶς αὐτοῦ ἐγένετο οὐδὲ ἕν[33] ὃ γέγονεν (4) ἐν αὐτῷ ζωὴ ἦν καὶ ἡ ζωὴ ἦν τὸ φῶς τῶν ἀνθρώπων.

The textual problem is whether ὃ γέγονεν marks the end of vs. 3 or the beginning of vs. 4.[34] The more or less traditional punctuation understands ὃ γέγονεν as concluding vs. 3, and the less popular punctuation takes it as the beginning of vs. 4. Thus we have the possibility of what we shall call

Reading I[35]

(3) πάντα δι' αὐτοῦ ἐγένετο καὶ χωρὶς αὐτοῦ ἐγένετο οὐδὲ ἕν ὃ γέγονεν. (4) ἐν αὐτῷ ζωὴ ἦν καὶ ἡ ζωὴ ἦν τὸ φῶς τῶν ἀνθρώπων.

(3) All things came into being through him, and apart from him came into being not one thing which has come into being. (4) In him was life and the life was the light of men.

and

Reading II

(3) πάντα δι' αὐτοῦ ἐγένετο καὶ χωρὶς αὐτοῦ ἐγένετο οὐδὲ ἕν. ὃ γέγονεν (4) ἐν αὐτῷ ζωὴ ἦν καὶ ἡ ζωὴ ἦν τὸ φῶς τῶν ἀνθρώπων.

---

[31] One should note too I. de la Potterie, "De Interpunctione et Interpretatione Versuum Joh. 1:3-4," *VD*, 33 (1955), pp. 193ff.

[32] Aland, "Eine Untersuchung zu Joh. 1:3-4," p. 209.

[33] We reserve for later the further question about the readings οὐδὲ ἕν/οὐδέν.

[34] For a tidy review of this central problem and related issues, see Brown's survey of the "five very difficult problems" in vs. 4a, in *The Gospel according to John*, I, pp. 6f.

[35] This labelling is exactly opposite to Aland's ("Eine Untersuchung zu Joh. 1:3-4," p. 85). It seems best to me to contrast the most familiar reading as *Reading I*, with the less familiar and more problematic reading as *Reading II*.

(3) All things came into being through him, and apart from him came into being not one thing. That which has come into being (4) in him was life and the life was the light of men.

Already, two problems must be mentioned in relation to *Reading II*. First, the meaning of ὃ γέγονεν here is very difficult. It will become apparent soon enough that this is in fact a crucial question and the source of the whole problem. In a way, our entire study will be an attempt to identify the original intent of this expression and to draw out its theological and literary implications. For the moment, I have tried to render it in the most straightforward and unprejudiced manner possible. The second problem in *Reading II* lies with the decision whether to place a comma after ἐν αὐτῷ, or earlier, after ὃ γέγονεν. The first yields what we may call *Reading II-A*: "That which has come into being in him, was life. . . ." The second alternative yields *Reading II-B*: "That which has come into being, in him (or "in it") was life. . . ." The distinction may otherwise be represented as the difference between (*Reading II-A*) "That-which-has-come-into-being-in-him was life. . . ." and (*Reading II-B*) "That-which-has-come-into-being in him (or "in it") was life. . . ." Generally, the distinction between *Reading I* and *Reading II* will suffice for the problems at hand, though at certain points the variations on *Reading II* (*Reading II-A* and *Reading II-B*) will have to be recalled and introduced.[36]

Our first task, taken up in Chapter I, will be to resolve, as well as possible, the textual question. Certainty is never attainable in such matters, but a strong case can be made for the originality of *Reading II*. The case will revolve around linguistic considerations of style and usage, and textual-critical considerations of the passage as it is represented in the Fathers, the Uncials, and P[66] and P[75].

The interpretation of *Reading II* is, however, far from clear. In Chapter II we will argue, in fact, that the misunderstanding of and misappropriation (probably in certain Arian circles) of the passage was responsible for the competing readings in the first place. In our own attempt to explain the text (*Reading II* = ὃ γέγονεν now taken with what follows it) we shall assign to it a sense which, though we believe it to be the author's own, has been generally overlooked: ὃ γέγονεν ἐν αὐτῷ ζωὴ ἦν καὶ ἡ ζωὴ ἦν τὸ φῶς τῶν ἀνθρώπων is a reference to the life-giving and light-imparting incarnation of the Logos. In order to make this case we will have to argue against the several attempts which, to make sense of *Reading II*, take ὃ

---

[36] For the sake of completeness, a fourth possible punctuation should be mentioned: (3) πάντα δι' αὐτοῦ ἐγένετο καὶ χωρὶς αὐτοῦ ἐγένετο οὐδὲ ἓν ὃ γέγονεν (4) ἐν αὐτῷ. ζωὴ ἦν καὶ ἡ ζωὴ ἦν τὸ φῶς τῶν ἀνθρώπων. But this punctuation barely occurs in the tradition and commands no claim to authority.

γέγονεν in vs. 4a as being in various ways a continuation or extension of the πάντα in vs. 3 (something like, "that (creation) which has come into being through him"). But then, and more constructively, we will have to provide evidence for our own interpretation according to which the perfect tense ὃ γέγονεν signals a movement, logically and temporally, to the historical incarnation of the Logos (something like, "what has (now) come about through him").

In Chapter III it will be shown that from our interpretation of *Reading II* clear implications follow immediately both for the logical-literary structure and the theological perspective of vss. 1-5. These verses contain a complete Logos hymn, falling into four distinct sections, each with its own logical center of gravity but following in logical succession upon the preceding one, and, on the theological side, spanning the four-fold progression of the Logos in his pre-existent relation to God, his creative relation to the cosmos, his incarnate saving relation to men, and—from John's standpoint—his present and continuing victorious relation to evil. Whether one views such a scheme as *"Heilsgeschichte"* is not important. What is important is that the perspective, whatever one may call it, is present in and proclaimed by this hymn which is the central stuff of the Prologue, which itself surely signals in some important way or ways the theology of the whole Fourth Gospel.

CHAPTER ONE

THE TEXT

No one questions the absolute necessity of the textual critic's labor and its logical priority over all else. Certainly the text-critical task is unavoidable here where everything depends on the proper reading of John 1:3/4, or, more specifically, the determination of whether ὃ γέγονεν concludes the thought of vs. 3 or begins the thought of vs. 4. The reader may wish to skip or skim over the present chapter, but its necessity and priority in the work should be evident.

The Status of the Problem

The status of the problem may be suggested in the following. *Reading II*,[1]

(3) πάντα δι' αὐτοῦ ἐγένετο καὶ χωρὶς αὐτοῦ ἐγένετο οὐδὲ ἕν. ὃ γέγονεν (4) ἐν αὐτῷ ζωὴ ἦν καὶ ἡ ζωὴ ἦν τὸ φῶς τῶν ἀνθρώπων.

was almost universally preferred among the earlier Fathers, but was dropped in the fourth century in favor of *Reading I*,

(3) πάντα δι' αὐτοῦ ἐγένετο καὶ χωρὶς αὐτοῦ ἐγένετο οὐδὲ ἕν ὃ γέγονεν. (4) ἐν αὐτῷ ζωὴ ἦν καὶ ἡ ζωὴ ἦν τὸ φῶς τῶν ἀνθρώπων.

Reading I was given boosts especially by the Vulgate and Erasmus' edition of the Greek New Testament and has hardened into the more or less traditional reading of texts and translations both.[2] More recently, however, *Reading II* has once again made a claim to originality.

Modern commentators on the passage tend to be split fairly evenly between the two readings. It is fairly representative to say that *Reading I* is preferred by B. Weiss, Zahn, Lagrange, Hirsch, A. Schlatter, Barrett, Haenchen, Jeremias, Demke, Feuillet, Schnackenburg, Morris, Borgen, Rissi, Schulz, Schmithals, and Mateos/Barreto. *Reading II* is accepted by Westcott, Loisy, Bernard, Gächter, Bultmann, Hoskyns/Davey, Boismard, Lacan, Sanders/Martin, de la Potterie, Lightfoot/Evans,

---

[1] Again, setting aside for the moment the further textual problem with οὐδὲ ἕν in vs. 3, as well as with the first (and sometimes also second) ἦν of vs. 4.

[2] For a history of the issue to the twentieth century, see I. de la Potterie, "De Punctuatie en de Exegese van Joh. 1:3-4 in de Traditie," *Bijdragen*, 16 (1955), pp. 117ff.

Lamarche, Brown, van den Bussche, Aland, Vawter, Lindars, Zimmermann, Gese, and Theobald.

Perhaps more important for the textual question are the judgments reflected in the most important editions of the Greek New Testament. The domination until recently of *Reading I* was insured by Erasmus' adoption of it in his edition of 1516, and, of the most important editors of the modern period, its adoption by Tischendorf (through his seventh edition), Weiss, Souter (in the editions of both 1910 and 1947), Merk, Bover, Vogels (first and second editions), and in the first twenty-five editions of the Nestle text. A reemergence of *Reading II* is reflected by its adoption in the editions of Barton, Lachmann, Tischendorf's eighth edition, Tregelles, Westcott-Hort, von Soden, Vogels' third edition, *The Greek-English Diglot*, Tasker, the *Greek New Testament* of the United Bible Societies, and its appearance in the twenty-sixth edition of Nestle/Aland. It is clear, then, that *Reading II* is regaining the ascendancy. It is difficult, however, to dislodge familiar readings from translations (a kind of "text-lag"), and *Reading I* continues to rule in the pulpit and pew as is evident from the fact that of the major English translations, only the *New English Bible* and the *Jerusalem Bible* adopt *Reading II*. The *American Standard Version* and the *Revised Standard Version* give *Reading II* as an alternative reading in a footnote.

Linguistic Evidence for Reading II

Before we consider the question from a strictly *textual* standpoint (involving manuscript witnesses, etc.), it should be noted that attempts have been made to decide between *Reading I* and *Reading II* on *linguistic* grounds, that is, on the basis of various literary, stylistic, and grammatical factors. Such attempts often concern the poetry, meter, and structure of the Logos hymn, specifically the "staircase" parallelism, the length of clauses, and the like; in addition, our attention is called to the supposed redundancy of *Reading I*, John's frequent use of ἐν at the beginning of sentences, his frequent use of οὐδέν at the end of sentences, the grammar of the passage, and so forth. Treatments of this linguistic-type evidence may be found here and there among the commentators,[3] but the treatment is always slight and it behooves us to take up these considerations more systematically and critically.

(i) In favor of *Reading II*, some have observed that vss. 1-5 involve a recurring pattern of expression, already noted in our preliminary com-

---

[3] For example, C. K. Barrett, *The Gospel according to St. John*, second ed. (Philadelphia: Westminster Press, 1978), pp. 156f., and Boismard, *Le Prologue de Saint Jean*, pp. 25ff.

ments,[4] in which the last element of a clause becomes the first element of the clause following it in "staircase" fashion (A→B, B→C, C→D), and that this pattern would require taking ὃ γέγονεν as connected with the previous ἐγένετο(s) of vs. 3 and extending the thought "upward" at vs. 4. For example, Brown: ". . . the poetry of the prologue favors our division [*Reading II*], for the climactic or 'staircase' parallelism of the lines requires that the end of one line should match the beginning of the next."[5] Boismard likewise sees *Reading II* as continuing this pattern of "mots-crochets," as he calls them,[6] whereby "la pensée semble ainsi s'élever puissamment, comme en un vol circulaire."[7] And de la Potterie calls this construction a "concatenatio tam caracteristica versuum in initio prologi" which would be preserved only on *Reading II*.[8]

It is true that this "staircase" pattern is more or less characteristic of vss. 1-5, and it is employed strictly and consistently in vs. 1 and vss. 4-5. But in fact this pattern gives way in vs. 2, and it could be argued that it is not taken up again until the ἐν αὐτῷ of vs. 4 on the grounds that the latter would allow the two series of staircases in vs. 1 and vss. 4-5 to get off on the same foot, namely, ἐν (= *Reading I*).[9] There is another difficulty with the "staircase" argument for *Reading II*. In order for the staircase connection to apply to vss. 3-4, what begins vs. 4 should be linguistically identical (or nearly so) with what concludes vs. 3. Certainly this is the case in vs. 1 (→λόγος, λόγος→θεόν, θεός→)[10] and in vss. 4-5 (→ζωή, ζωή→φῶς, φῶς→σκοτία, σκοτία→). But the γέγονεν which is taken as beginning vs. 4 is hardly the same form as the ἐγένετο of vs. 3. More important, aside from the dissimilarity of the forms involved, the *thought* must at least coincide, which means that ὃ γέγονεν must be a kind of restatement of the πάντα of vs. 3. We shall see later that though this (i.e. ὃ γέγονεν = πάντα) is a very common interpretation, it is to be rejected. It will become one of our central theses, in fact, that on *Reading II* ὃ γέγονεν

---

[4] See above, p. 8.

[5] Brown, *The Gospel according to John*, I, p. 6.

[6] Boismard, *Le Prologue de Saint Jean*, p. 28.

[7] Boismard, *Le Prologue de Saint Jean*, p. 16. He adds that this is why "dès le temps de saint Irénée, le symbolisme de l'aigle en plein vol montant vers le ciel, fut attribué à saint Jean."

[8] De la Potterie, "De Interpunctione et Interpretatione Versuum Joh. 1:3-4," p. 204. He cites Erasmus who said that this type of construction "congruit enim hujus Evangelistae peculiari sermoni" and that it results in *Reading II* (*Annotationes in Novum Testamentum* (Basel, 1542), p. 237). Cf. also Bultmann, who calls this a "kettenartige Verschlingung der Sätze" (*Das Evangelium Johannes*, p. 2) which requires *Reading II* (p. 21, n. 2)

[9] Cf. Richter's thesis about ἐν as a "strukturbildendes Element," discussed below.

[10] Though in the Introduction we conjectured that vs. 1c (as well as vs. 2) is not actually a part of the original Logos hymn.

does not refer in any way to creation, but to something quite new and different. If, indeed, we are correct in this then the staircase argument may be entirely irrelevant here. For on either *Reading I* or *Reading II* a completely new thought is inaugurated at vs. 4, and one could expect also a new series of staircase connections as easily on one reading as the other.

(ii) Against *Reading I* many have observed that ὃ γέγονεν construed with vs. 3 results in a pointless redundancy, all the more conspicuous in light of the care taken in both the thought and expression of these lines. Loisy, for example, condemns it as being neither an explanation nor an emphasis, but a mere pleonasm,[11] and Lacan calls it a "redondance choquante" which "ôte au stique 3b sa sobre vigueur."[12] But, first, Barrett has argued for *Reading I* precisely on the grounds of John's "frequent repetitiousness" such as is found already in vss. 1-2.[13] More important, if the lines before us do in fact bear a poetic and structured imprint, then it should not be surprising that a redundancy occurs, even artificially, for the purposes, say, of rounding out a line. Related to this last is Rissi's observation that the pleonastic οὐδὲ ἕν ὃ γέγονεν may reflect a typically liturgical use of language.[14] Morris thinks that *Reading I* results in a "terse forceful statement" and that taking ὃ γέγονεν with vs. 3 is "natural and adds to the emphasis that is there built up."[15] Still more important, it must be asked whether we have here a redundancy at all. Aside from the fact that a true redundancy would require not ὃ γέγονεν but ὃ ἐγένετο, Morris notes that in fact the aorist ἐγένετο and the perfect γέγονεν involve two different ideas: πάντα ἐγένετο signifies the original creation whereas ὃ γέγονεν signifies the continuing and present creation.[16] The shift from the aorist ἐγένετο to the perfect ὃ γέγονεν is certainly significant, but we ourselves will go even further than Morris and argue that ὃ γέγονεν refers in no way to creation, though our view will be seen to rest on *Reading II*.

[11] Alfred Loisy, *Le Quatrième Évangile*, second ed. (Paris: Nourry, 1921), p. 92.
[12] Lacan, "L'Oeuvre du Verbe Incarné," p. 62. Cf. also B. F. Westcott, *The Gospel according to St. John* (Grand Rapids, Mich.: Eerdmans, 1978 (orig. 1880)), p. 30; Bernard, *A Critical and Exegetical Commentary on the Gospel of St. John*, I, p. 3.
[13] Barrett, *The Gospel according to St. John*, p. 157. But, of course, and contrary to many exegetes, vs. 2 contains a new thought over against what has been said in vs. 1: It was in the *beginning* that the Word was with God. Oddly, Barrett himself emphasizes this: "This is not mere repetition" (p. 156).
[14] Rissi, "Die Logoslieder im Prolog des vierten Evangeliums," p. 326, n. 30.
[15] Leon Morris, *The Gospel according to John* (Grand Rapids, Mich.: Eerdmans, 1971), p. 82.
[16] Morris, *The Gospel according to John*, p. 80. Thus the problem that J. N. Sanders and B. A. Mastin see is not as severe as they think: "To translate [ὃ γέγονεν] as if it were a past tense, 'that was made,' is a misrepresentation which must, however, be accepted if the clause is read as part of the previous verse" (*A Commentary on the Gospel of St. John* (London: Black, 1968), p. 71).

(iii) Somewhat has been made, too, of the rhythm of the clauses resulting from the different readings. Gächter argued for *Reading I* on the basis of "Tonwörter": Both *Reading II-A* and *Reading II-B* yield an unrhythmic line of only one stressed word.[17] But Gächter's decisions about what the "Tonwörter" are appear to be very subjective, and, in any case, the sort of rhythm involved here is surely not that of meter or stress, but reflects rather the more semitic interest in the balance of the lines relative to one another and this means especially their length. In favor of *Reading I*, Rissi finds the length of the second member of vs. 3 on *Reading I* not particularly conspicuous "bei freiem Rhythmus."[18] Schnackenburg thinks that from considerations of rhythm and structure nothing decisive follows at all: On *Reading II* vs. 3 is a good distich; on *Reading I* it is a good tristich.[19] But most of those who have taken up the question of rhythm here have correctly seen in it an evidence for *Reading II*—for example Loisy, de la Potterie, Boismard, Bultmann, and Aland.[20] The rhythm of these verses (Boismard emphasizes especially the "perfect parallelism" in vs. 3) is broken if the words ὃ γέγονεν are taken with what precedes, that is, *Reading I*: Verse 3 becomes too long, and by virtue of an addition that in fact adds nothing to the sense (recall the redundancy argument just mentioned), and vs. 4 is made to begin with a certain abruptness; on *Reading II*, however, both vs. 3 and vs. 4 are composed of two members of approximately the same length.

(iv) The rhythm argument may, however, be even stronger than it first appears in light of certain external evidence bearing on the structure of vs. 3. By now we are used to the idea that John 1:1-5 bears every mark of a planned and polished piece, and this may be especially so in the case of vs. 3 where we seem to have, as Boismard says, a perfect *parallelismus membrorum*:

πάντα δι' αὐτοῦ ἐγένετο,
καὶ χωρὶς αὐτοῦ ἐγένετο οὐδὲ ἕν.

Boismard refines the device here employed by John:

Ce verset est composé de deux phrases successives, simplement liées par la conjonction "et." Selon un procédé couramment employé dans la littérature juive, le parallélisme antithétique, la deuxième phrase reprend, sous forme négative, l'idée exprimée dans la première, avec toutefois une nuance qu'il importera de dégager.[21]

---

[17] Gächter, "Strophen im Johannesevangelium," pp. 101f.
[18] Rissi, "Die Logoslieder im Prolog des vierten Evangeliums," p. 322.
[19] Schnackenburg, *Das Johannesevangelium*, I, p. 216.
[20] Loisy, *Le Quatrième Évangile*, p. 92; de la Potterie, "De Interpunctione et Interpretatione Versuum Joh. 1:3-4," p. 204; Boismard, *Le Prologue de Saint Jean*, pp. 28f.; Bultmann, *Das Evangelium des Johannes*, p. 21, n. 2; Aland, "Eine Untersuchung zu Joh. 1:3-4," p. 206.
[21] Boismard, *Le Prologue de Saint Jean*, p. 22.

But it is his observation that this "parallélisme antithétique" was "couramment employé dans la littérature juive" that is especially relevant here. P. Braun has pointed out,[22] and de la Potterie has further emphasized,[23] the striking similarity of John 1:3,

> All things came into being through him,
> And apart from him nothing came into being.

and certain passages in the Dead Sea manuscripts, a literature with which, as de la Potterie observes, "vocabularium Sancti Johannis . . . non paucas affinitates habet."[24] For example,[25].

> By his knowledge have all things been made,
> And all things which are, he has established by his own counsel,
> And without him not [anything] comes to be.
>   (*Manual of Discipline*, XI, 11)
>
> For without you the way is not complete,
> And without your good-pleasure nothing comes to be . . .
> And all things that have been made, have been made in your good-pleasure.
>   (*Manual of Discipline*, XI, 17-18)
>
> Through your design all things have been made.
> And by the counsel of your heart you have established all things;
> And without you not any thing comes to be,
> And without your good-pleasure not anything comes to be.
>   (*Hymns*, X, 1-2)

John 1:3 thus not only expresses the widespread Judaic sentiment of the universality of creation by God, but precisely by means of the same positive/negative formula found in the passages quoted above. The sentiment is, loosely,

> All things come to be through God,
> And without him nothing comes to be.

In this formula the additional relative clause, "which has come into being," has no place and thus in John 1:3 the additional ὃ γέγονεν might

---

[22] F.-M. Braun, "L'Arrière-fond Judaïque du Quatrième Évangile et la Communauté de l'Alliance," *RB*, 62 (1955), p. 15.

[23] De la Potterie, "De Interpunctione et Interpretatione Versuum Joh. 1:3-4," pp. 204ff. Cf. also Schnackenburg, *Das Johannesevangelium*, I, p. 214.

[24] De la Potterie, "De Interpunctione et Interpretatione Versuum Joh. 1:3-4," p. 204.

[25] My translation of de la Potterie's Latin rendering ("De Interpunctione et Interpretatione Versuum Joh. 1:3-4," p. 205). The Hebrew is at points fragmentary.

have sounded to the Jewish ear an awkward intrusion—a vote against *Reading I*.

(v) For a resolution of the problem Haacker has appealed to a literary world quite different from that of the Dead Sea. He sees in certain Egyptian creation-texts (known from temple inscriptions) a recurring construction, in both positive and negative forms, similar to the creation formula of John 1:3 when ὃ γέγονεν is included. One of Haacker's four cited passages: (Der Gott Thot) "der entstand, als noch nicht entstanden war, was [dann] entstand . . ., der Eine, der dies Alles machte." From such he concludes boldly in favor of *Reading I*,[26] and with the approval of Borgen.[27] But aside from the fact that parallels to anything may always be found if one is willing to travel far enough, it requires some imagination to see the parallelism that Haacker and Borgen see between the cited Egyptian texts and John 1:3 (*Reading I*) and, in any event, the former can hardly be as relevant as similarities found within Jewish literature, such as those Dead Sea parallelisms cited above.

(vi) Some, for example Barrett, have reasoned in favor of *Reading I* on the grounds that John frequently begins a sentence with ἐν.[28] It is true that in seventeen instances (excluding the present passage) John introduces a sentence with ἐν, and it is at least relevant that this is the case (excluding the present passage) two times in the Prologue: vss. 1 and 10. Richter, moreover, has attempted to show that in the Logos Hymn ἐν is a "formales Gliederungsprinzip" and "strukturbildendes Element" which signals the beginning of three strophes (vss. 1, 3; 4-5; 10-12b).[29] Schnackenburg, too, believes that ἐν αὐτῷ marks the beginning of the second strophe and turns our attention from creation to the world of men with a new affirmation about the Logos.[30]

But to these observations it may be countered that out of more than two hundred instances of ἐν in John, the seventeen instances (excluding the present passage) in which it begins a sentence is doubtfully a strong enough statistic on the basis of which to generalize about a stylistic trait. For that matter, it is not uncommon, either, for John to begin sentences with relative pronouns, as he does in the Prologue itself at least once (aside from vs. 4, *Reading II*) at vs. 12 (which many include in the original Logos hymn). Richter's reasoning about ἐν as a "strukturbildendes Ele-

---

[26] Klaus Haacker, "Eine formgeschichtliche Beobachtung zu Joh. 1:3 fin.," *BZ*, 12 (1968), pp. 119ff.

[27] Peder Borgen, "Logos was the True Light," p. 126.

[28] Barrett, *The Gospel according to St. John*, p. 157.

[29] Georg Richter, "Ist ἐν ein strukturbildendes Element im Logoshymnus Joh. 1:1ff.?" *Biblica*, 51 (1970), pp. 539ff.

[30] Schnackenburg, *Das Johannesevangelium*, I, pp. 216f.

ment" in the Prologue of John, which, specifically, initiates a second strophe with vs. 4, must be reckoned with as a serious consideration. But if in fact it can be concluded on other grounds that ὅ γέγονεν begins vs. 4, then not only is the reading at vss. 3/4 thereby settled, but also Richter's thesis about ἐν as a "strukturbildendes Element" in the Prologue is significantly weakened. As for Schnackenburg's point, he assumes that ὅ γέγονεν must refer to creation, but we will argue at length in Chapter II that it does not refer to creation, and that the whole clause ὅ γέγονεν ἐν αὐτῷ begins the new affirmation about the Logos.

(vii) Closely related to the opinion that it is characteristic of John to begin clauses with ἐν is the view of Barrett and others that the expression ἐν αὐτῷ ζωὴ ἦν seems to be paralleled elsewhere in John, again favoring *Reading I*. Barrett cites 5:26 where it is said that the Father has given the Son ζωὴν ἔχειν ἐν ἑαυτῷ, 5:39 which declares that ἐν αὐταῖς (i.e. ταῖς γραφαῖς) is ζωή, and 6:53 according to which believers would not have ζωὴν ἐν ἑαυτοῖς if they did not partake of the flesh and blood of the Son of Man.[31]

With respect to the first of these alleged parallelisms, Aland has answered, perhaps weakly, that the context of 5:26 shows that it involves not an assertion about life being in the Son as much as the Son's equality with the Father. Against Barrett's citation of 5:39 and 6:53, Aland answers, more forcefully, that these involve no claim about the Logos, and it is more Johannine to represent the Logos as life itself rather than as *having* life, as in 6:33, 6:35, and especially 14:6. Likewise, if we include further John's application of φῶς to the Logos (and φῶς is, after all, equated in 1:4 with ζωή which in turn is said to be ἐν αὐτῷ) then 8:12 is relevant inasmuch as the Logos is represented not as *having* light but rather *being* the light.[32] Generally, Aland judges that by comparison with the literary and theological style of the preceding verses, *Reading I*, with its simple "in him was life," appears too facile and even banal. *Reading I* would have rather fitted the aggressive and majestic character of the preceding assertions concerning the Logos had it said, αὐτὸς (or ὁ λόγος) ζωὴ ἦν, "he (or the Logos) was life."[33] For our own part, we would suggest that the expressions cited by Barrett are hardly decisive as evidence for *Reading I* or even relevant. In the first place, one must decide whether in 1:4 the ἐν in ἐν αὐτῷ is positional or instrumental; if the latter, then the Barrett passages are quite beside the point. And in any case, on *either* interpretation of the ἐν, if it is appropriate to say of the Logos that ἐν αὐτῷ

---

[31] Barrett, *The Gospel according to St. John*, p. 157.
[32] Aland, "Eine Untersuchung zu Joh. 1:3-4," p. 205.
[33] Aland, "Eine Untersuchung zu Joh. 1:3-4," pp. 204f.

ζωὴ ἦν (*Reading I*), is it any less appropriate to say with respect to the Logos that ὃ γέγονεν ἐν αὐτῷ ζωὴ ἦν (*Reading II*), at least with the meaning which we will argue later, "What appeared in him was life"?

(viii) While it is sometimes argued that *Reading I* is supported by John's characteristic use of ἐν at the beginning of sentences, it may easily be argued, in support of *Reading II*, that it is also characteristic of John to end sentences or clauses with various forms of οὐδείς. In fact, sentences or clauses ending with some form of οὐδείς (usually οὐδέν or οὐδένα) occur in John almost as commonly as sentences or clauses beginning with ἐν, and it may be even more obviously a stylistic trait in view of its distinctiveness over against the more general ἐν-plus-some-dative-or-other. Though we leave until later the textual question as to οὐδέν vs. οὐδὲ ἕν, we may here anticipate that in all probability οὐδὲ ἕν is the original reading. If so, οὐδὲ ἕν occurs in John only twice, at 1:3 and at (according to the best witnesses) 3:27, but should be construed with the closely related οὐδέν, οὐδένα, etc. as being the more emphatic expression. Further, the concluding and emphatic οὐδὲ ἕν, far from being gramatically intolerable as Zahn thought,[34] would appear to be clearly suited to a conclusion and was often so employed as many instances from Classical and Hellenistic Greek show.[35] To this it might be added that from a rhetorical standpoint the alternative οὐδὲ ἕν ὃ γέγονεν issues in something of an anticlimactic let-down. In any event, if one believes, for grammatical-stylistic reasons, that vs. 3 concluded with οὐδὲ ἕν, then this is obviously evidence for *Reading II*. But it should be noted too that even on the reading οὐδέν, *Reading II* may derive some support, for following οὐδέν one would expect, on *Reading I*, not ὃ γέγονεν, but ὅ τι γέγονεν.[36]

(ix) It has been suggested also that the placing of ὃ γέγονεν may be understood in terms of the following imperfects: ἐν αὐτῷ ζωὴ ἦν καὶ ἡ ζωὴ ἦν τὸ φῶς. Adolf Schlatter, for example, reasoned that ὃ γέγονεν taken with vs. 4 (*Reading II*) would have required present tenses in what follows, and that this is in fact how the present-tense ἐστίν, which does appear in some manuscript witnesses in place of the first ἦν, and sometimes the second ἦν also, arose.[37] But it is equally plausible—later, in our discussion of the textual evidence, we shall argue that it is much more plausible—that the

---

[34] Theodor Zahn, *Das Evangelium des Johannes*, fifth and sixth eds. (Leipzig: Deichert, 1921), pp. 52f.
[35] So Bultmann, who provides examples (*Das Evangelium des Johannes*, p. 20, n. 1). Cf. also Walter Bauer, *Das Johannesevangelium*, second ed. (Tübingen: Mohr, 1925), p. 11.
[36] Thus Schnackenburg, *Das Johannesevangelium*, I, p. 216.
[37] Adolf Schlatter, *Der Evangelist Johannes: Wie er Spricht, Denkt und Glaubt,* (Stuttgart: Calwer, 1930), p. 6.

later ἐστίν is evidence of a straining attempt to accommodate the *already accepted* perfect ὃ γέγονεν as the beginning of vs. 4.

(x) Still another line of consideration is opened up by Loisy who takes ὃ γέγονεν with vs. 4 as required for a certain parallelism he sees there: "That which has come to be, in it was life" (*Reading II-B*) is a reference to the life that is in the human race, and the following line, "the life was the light of men," is a restatement of this thought.[38] The big difficulty, of course, is seeing in ὃ γέγονεν a reference to men, even in view of Loisy's alleged parallelism. On the more linguistic side, *Reading II-B*, necessary as it is for Loisy's interpretation, must prove itself over the more natural *Reading II-A*, and even on *Reading II-B*, the interpretation of the pronoun αὐτῷ as a neuter "it," also necessary for Loisy's view, must prove itself over a masculine "him."

(xi) In fact, however, Gese finds support for *Reading II* precisely because it *can* yield *Reading II-B* with its "im Hebräischen beliebte Casus-pendens-Konstruction."[39] But whether this anacoluthic construction (which begins with one subject and immediately changes to another) is popular with Hebrew is not as relevant as whether it is popular with John. It is true that John elsewhere employs this construction, as in the Prologue itself at vss. 12 and 18, and in many instances beyond the Prologue as at 15:2 and 17:2, 24 (the last is especially relevant inasmuch as it involves a neuter relative pronoun plus a perfect tense), but it is something of an overstatement to say with Loisy that "rien n'est plus familier" to John than such a construction.[40] And, be that as it may, at John 1:4a it remains an awkward and troublesome one, as we will see at many points later.

(xii) To all of this may be added the question whether, on *Reading I*, the phrase ὃ γέγονεν is even grammatical. Both Bultmann and Gese (who favor *Reading II*) and even Schnackenburg (who favors *Reading I*) agree that on *Reading I* we ought to have, rather, οὐδὲ ἓν ὧν γέγονεν (or after οὐδὲν, ὅ τι γέγονεν).[41] Haenchen, on the other hand, thinks that the more classical ὧν γέγονεν would be foreign to the *koine* Greek of John.[42] This is to say nothing of Burney's proposal that the relative ὃ is a mistranslation of an underlying Aramaic *dᵉ*—according to Burney, who opts for *Reading II*, the meaning of the original Aramaic was, "Because in him was

---

[38] Loisy, *Le Quartrième Évangile*, pp. 92f.

[39] Gese, "Der Johannesprolog," p. 162.

[40] Loisy, *Le Quatrième Évangile*, p. 92.

[41] Bultmann, *Das Evangelium des Johannes*, p. 21, n. 2; Gese, "Der Johannesprolog," p. 162.; Schnackenburg, *Das Johannesevangelium*, I, p. 216. Cf. also Bauer, *Das Johannesevangelium*, p. 11, and Barrett, *The Gospel according to St. John*, p. 156.

[42] Haenchen, "Probleme des johanneischen 'Prologs,' " p. 316, n. 51.

life."[43] Aside from certain critical observations that may be raised on this latter point,[44] theses about an Aramaic document underlying the Fourth Gospel and/or Prologue are now generally rejected, and, in any case, a resolution of the grammatical question cannot be found here, for whatever an alleged original Aramaic document may have said, the translator clearly intended to write ὃ γέγονεν.

These then are the usual arguments of a "linguistic" sort which have been raised for and against the two readings. Understandably, one might discover nothing decisive in such considerations inasmuch as the arguments tend to cancel themselves out. Nonetheless, our own impression, and it can hardly be more than an impression, is that the balance of such evidence weighs somewhat in favor of *Reading II*. Especially relevant, in our view, is John's use of οὐδὲ ἕν (or οὐδέν) at the end of sentences, the empty (or at least nearly empty) repetition involved in *Reading I*, and the more balanced rhythm (that is, length of lines) resulting from *Reading II*. In the end, however, the best evidence for the original reading must be, if possible, not linguistic but textual, and to that evidence we turn now.

The Textual Evidence for Reading II

From a purely textual standpoint it appears that there is hardly a problem. Lindars, for example, marshalls the textual evidence and then announces that "the external support for [*Reading II*] is thus overwhelming..."[45] Even in 1881, long before the discovery of P[75], Westcott judged that "it would be difficult to find a more complete consent of ancient authorities of favour of any reading, than that which supports [*Reading II*]."[46]

It may be useful at the start to provide a list of the two readings as found in the most important MSS., Versions, and Fathers.[47]

---

[43] Charles Fox Burney, *The Aramaic Origin of the Fourth Gospel* (Oxford, England: Oxford University Press, 1922), p. 29.

[44] See Matthew Black, *An Aramaic Approach to the Gospels and Acts*, third ed. (Oxford, England: Clarendon Press, 1967), p. 75, and Fredric W. Schlatter, "The Problem of Jn. 1:3b-4a," *CBQ*, 34 (1972), pp. 54ff.

[45] Barnabas Lindars, *The Gospel of John* (London: Oliphants, 1972), p. 84.

[46] Westcott, *The Gospel according to St. John*, p. 4.

[47] These lists have been collated from the *criticus apparatus* of the United Bible Societies' *Greek New Testament* and from Aland ("Eine Untersuchung zu Joh. 1:3-4," pp. 188ff.), though they reflect our own and differing judgment at certain points. We reflect here only the essential difference between the two readings and not further variations such as οὐδὲ ἕν/οὐδέν or the subsequent ἦν/ἐστίν. The notation (*, suppl, c, etc.) conforms to that of the *Greek New Testament*.

Reading I:

MSS.	6th/7th cent.	$\aleph^c$
	9th cent.	050^c
		U
		063
	10th cent.	X
		Γ
	9th-15th cent.	f^1
		f^{13}
		33
		565
		1009
		1010
		1079
		1216
		1230
		1242
		1253
		1344
		1365
		1546
		1646
	5th-17th cent.	Byz Lect
Versions	2nd/3rd-7th cent.	$syr^{p,h}$
	3rd-4th cent.	cop^{bo}
	4th cent.	vg^{cl}
	4th/5th cent.	arm
	5th cent.	geo
Fathers	3rd cent.	Adamantius
	4th cent.	Alexander
		Ephraem
		Ambrose (1/3)
		Didymus
		Epiphanius
		Chrysostom
	5th cent.	Jerome
		Nonnus
		Ps-Ignatius

Reading II:

MSS.	c. 200	P^{75}
	5th cent.	C
	5th/6th cent.	D*
	7th cent.	W^{suppl}
	9th cent.	U*
		050*
		Λ
Versions	3rd/4th-7th cent.	$syr^{c,\ (pal)}$
	4th cent.	vg^{ww}
	3rd-6th cent.	$cop^{sa,fay}$
	5th cent.	it^b

Fathers	2nd cent.	Theodotus[acc to Clement]
		Valentinians[acc to Irenaeus and Clement]
		Irenaeus
		Diateresson[i,n]
		Ptolemy
		Heracleon
		Theophilus
		Naassenes
	3rd cent.	Perateni
		Clement
		Tertullian
		Hippolytus
		Origen
		Eusebius
	4th cent.	Ambrosiaster
		Hilary
		Athanasius
		Cyril-Jerusalem
		Ambrose (2/3)
		Epiphanius
	5th cent.	Augustine
		Cyril

In addition to those listed above, a number of MSS. give what might be called a "double punctuation" or even a "multiple punctuation" of our passage, that is, some combination of minor stops (*hypostigmai*) or major stops (*teleiai stigmai*).[48] Two minor stops are given in L (eighth century) though ὃ γέγονεν is given a capital ῞Ο, and in F (ninth century). A full stop followed by a minor stop is given in E, Ψ, and 047 (eighth century), G, H, Y, Π, Θ, K, V, M, and ω though it begins ἐν αὐτῷ with a capital ᾽Ε (ninth century), and S (tenth century).[49] O and 211 (eighth century) enigmatically include three pauses: οὐδὲ ἕν. ὃ. γέγονεν. ἐν αὐτῷ ζωὴ ἦν; but-these are outdone by Δ which gives *four*: οὐδὲ ἓν ὃ. γέγονεν. ἐν. αὐτῷ. ζωὴ ἦν. 0141[c] (tenth century) strikes out ὃ γέγονεν entirely, thereby striking out the problem! (The latter instances illustrate the hopeless state to which the problem sometimes sank.) Conspicuous by their absence from our lists are some of the most important MSS.: P[66] (*c.* 200), B and ℵ* (fourth century), and A (fifth century); these early MSS. provide no punctuation of the passage at all.

A glance over our lists produces the following general impression: The best punctuated MSS. give *Reading II*; the Versions tend to be split between *Reading I* and *Reading II*; the Fathers prefer *Reading II* by a large majority. In a word, the weight of textual witnesses favors *Reading II*.

---

[48] These have been identified from Aland's list ("Eine Untersuchung zu Joh. 1:3-4," pp. 188f.).

[49] Inasmuch as all of these give a major stop before ὃ γέγονεν, it would be possible to consider them as evidence for *Reading II*.

Three lines of comment are required concerning (i) the witnesses of the Fathers, (ii) the uncials, and (iii) P⁶⁶ and P⁷⁵.

(i) Quite to the contrary of Lamarche who discounted the relevance of the Fathers' witness to our passage,⁵⁰ it is even more relevant than one might have thought.⁵¹

Lamarche agreed with Theodore of Mopsuestia that a quotation of vs. 3 which pauses or concludes after οὐδὲ ἕν proves nothing: The author, unsure of the ending of vs. 3 or the beginning or meaning of vs. 4, simply avoids quoting it. On this reasoning it does not follow, for example, that Tertullian may be aligned as a witness to *Reading II* on the grounds that he ends with οὐδὲ ἕν.⁵² But this conclusion is rightly rejected by Aland who holds Lamarche to account for his failure to heed properly the chronological relation (indeed, disparity) of the Fathers by lumping them all together, and his injustice to the contexts of the quotations. When these precautions are taken, it is usually possible to decide whether a quotation is complete or abbreviated. This is the case, for example, with Irenaeus, Tertullian, Clement, and Origen. Each of them cite John 1:3, 1:4, or 1:3-4 numerous times and each of them clearly intends *Reading II*.⁵³

That Irenaeus, in quoting vs. 3 in its shorter form (*Reading II*), is not avoiding the question of the placing of ὃ γέγονεν is made clear from the fact that in some instances he quotes the whole of vss. 1-4 according to *Reading II*.⁵⁴ The case is similar in Tertullian who twice quotes vss. 1-3 in full (apparently).⁵⁵ Clement is important not only because of the breadth of his learning and culture, but also in view of the fact that in quoting our passage he alternates between ὃ γέγονεν ἐν αὐτῷ ζωὴ ἦν and ὃ γέγονεν ἐν αὐτῷ ζωὴ ἐστίν, though he never wavers over the placing of ὃ γέγονεν with vs. 4—the ambiguity over ἦν/ἐστίν had now set in, but not over ὃ γέγονεν. Neither can the fact that Origen quotes vs. 3 according to the shortened form (*Reading II*) be adduced as evidence for Lamarche's theory because (1) in one passage Origen explains the logic of the short version of vs. 3 (*Reading II*), namely, that if everything came into being through the Logos, then it must be that nothing came into being apart

---

⁵⁰ Nonetheless, see his useful survey: P. Lamarche, "Le Prologue de Jean," *RSR*, 52 (1964), pp. 514ff.
⁵¹ For much in the following paragraphs we are indebted to Aland, "Eine Untersuchung zu Joh. 1:3-4," pp. 190ff.
⁵² Lamarche, "Le Prologue de Jean," pp. 517f.
⁵³ Aland, "Eine Untersuchung zu Joh. 1:3-4," pp. 191ff. Aland provides complete documentation of the quotations and contexts.
⁵⁴ Cf. Irenaeus, *Adversus Haereses*, I, 8, 5, (*PG*, 7, 533); III, 11, 1 (*PG*, 7, 880).
⁵⁵ Tertullian, *Adversus Hermogenem*, XX (*PL*, 2, 240); *Adversus Praxean*, XXI (*PL*, 2, 203).

from him,[56] and (2) in any event in all of his quotations of vs. 4 he begins with ὃ γέγονεν (*Reading II*). It is, perhaps, decisive that while Origen otherwise freely employs different readings of a passage on different occasions, in this instance (John 1:3-4) he cites the passage repeatedly and exclusively according to *Reading II*. Origen did not know of any variation in this text.

But the force of the Fathers' witness to *Reading II* is even more striking when we take into account their total context, including their frequent apologetical intention in citing John 1:3-4. Irenaeus (for example in *Adversus Haereses*), Tertullian (*Adversus Hermogenem, Adversus Marcionem, De Resurrectione Mortuorum, Adversus Praxean*), and Origen (*In Ioannis Evangelium*) often cited John 1:3-4 in their struggle against the Gnostics' interpretation of the text.[57] We give here just one example from Irenaeus:

"πάντα δι' αὐτοῦ ἐγένετο, καὶ χωρὶς αὐτοῦ ἐγένετο οὐδ' ἕν·" πᾶσι γὰρ τοῖς μετ' αὐτὸν αἰῶσι μορφῆς καὶ γενέσεως αἴτιος ὁ λόγος ἐγένετο. ἀλλὰ "ὃ γέγονεν ἐν αὐτῷ," φησί, "ζωή ἐστιν·" ἐνθάδε καὶ συζυγίαν ἐμήνυσε· τὰ μὲν γὰρ ὅλα ἔφη δι' αὐτοῦ γεγενῆσθαι, τὴν δὲ ζωὴν ἐν αὐτῷ.[58]

In this remarkable passage Ireneaus quotes John 1:3-4 for the purpose of attacking and correcting a gnostic misinterpretation and abuse of it. What is striking in this and similar citations is that it is not the text of John 1:3-4 (*Reading II*) that is in question here, but rather the interpretation of the passage. There can be little doubt that Irenaeus would have here and elsewhere gladly employed as a counter-argument an alternate reading of this passage if he had known of one, and this same point is true of the apologetical citations of the passage in the other Fathers as well.[59]

Especially in view of this last consideration one must agree with Vawter that the argument from tradition (in this case the first three centuries) for *Reading II* is an "impressive" one:

Antecedently, it was unlikely that the early Greek Fathers and the later Western tradition would take the text as they did. There must have been a compelling reason, and that reason obviously did not arise from habit only or from simple convenience, since in this acceptation the text was always open to an heretical interpretation.[60]

---

[56] Origen, *In Ioannis Evangelium*, II, 13 (*PG*, XX, 148).

[57] For a brief survey of Gnostic interpretations of the first verses of John and especially vs. 4 (*Reading II*), see Haenchen, "Probleme des johanneischen 'Prologs,' " pp. 316ff.; also Elaine H. Pagels, *The Johannine Gospel in Gnostic Exegesis: Heracleon's Commentary on John* (Nashville, Tenn.: Abingdon Press, 1973), esp. Chs. 1 and 2, and Maurice F. Wiles, *The Spiritual Gospel: The Interpretation of the Fourth Gospel in the Early Church* (Cambridge, England: Cambridge University Press, 1960), pp. 96ff.

[58] Irenaeus, *Adversus Haereses*, I, 8, 5 (*PG* 7, 533).

[59] So Aland, "Eine Untersuchung zu Joh. 1:3-4," pp. 191f.

[60] Bruce Vawter, "What Came to Be in Him was Life (Jn. 1:3b-4a)," *CBQ* 25 (1963), p. 402.

The "compelling reason" must have been, of course, that *Reading II*, though problematic,[61] was in fact perceived as exclusive, universal, and fixed in the tradition—and unalterable.

On the other hand, note must be taken of Haenchen's view that *Reading I* was the original though the Fathers adopted *Reading II* under the influence of early Gnostic usage. After a survey of the various Gnostic employments of John 1:3-4 (*Reading II*) he asserts,

> Als die Grosskirche das zuerst von den Gnostikern dem "Johannes" zugeschriebene vierte Evangelium auslegte, behielt sie trotz aller Schwierigkeiten die gnostische Interpunktion bei.[62]

Schnackenburg too grants the possibility at least:

> Es ist leicht möglich, dass die Gnostiker mit ihrer Textabteilung vor ὃ γέγονεν die frühen Kirchenväter beeinflusst haben; die älteste LA braucht in diesem Falle nicht der ursprüngliche Text zu sein.[63]

But this view of the matter can hardly be sustained. First, it is much too speculative against the hard fact of the earliest textual witnesses. It is, of course, always possible that the earliest extant reading need not be the original, but one must be very cautious when flying in the face of the one concrete datum that one possesses. Further, we are asked to believe not only that for the large body of orthodox readers the change was from the *lectio proclivior* to the *lectio difficilior*, but that under Gnostic influence the *lectio proclivior* vanished without a trace. We recall here what was said above about the exclusive recognition of *Reading II* in Irenaeus, Tertullian, Clement, and especially Origen who wrote a commentary on John and who sooner or later employed practically every variant of the texts he quoted and who would surely have know of such an alternate reading (that is, *Reading I*) had there been one. Finally, the thesis in question is somewhat circular inasmuch as it presupposes that the Gnostic interpretation of the passage provided the impetus for *Reading II*, but that is at least part of what is in question here, and in any case it is no less difficult to demonstrate this than to believe that *Reading II* was original.

(ii)[64] It has already been noted that two of the most important uncials give no punctuation at all for our passage: ℵ* and B. In addition, the United Bible Societies' *Greek New Testament* correctly cites A also as giving

---

[61] For more about the heretical employment of John 1:4 (*Reading II*), see below, pp. 45ff., on the origin of *Reading I* as a defense against the Arian and Gnostic interpretations of *Reading II*.

[62] Haenchen, "Probleme des johanneischen 'Prologs,' " p. 319.

[63] Schnackenburg, *Das Johannesevangelium*, I, p. 216.

[64] The following discussion is adapted (with minor editing) from my article "Codex Bezae on John 1:3-4: One Dot or Two?" *TZ*, 32 (1976), pp. 269ff.

no punctuation, though it does favor ever so slightly *Reading II* inasmuch as it foregoes a space or two at the end of a line in order to begin a new line with ὃ γέγονεν.[65] But at any rate A is an inferior MS. for the Gospels. The situation with D (cited above as supporting *Reading II*) is more complicated, and a somewhat extended comment is in order.

The 5th/6th century Codex Bezae (D), as if we did not already have enough problems, has seemed to some to punctuate both before *and* after ὃ γέγονεν. We have seen that other MSS. too give this "double punctuation," but these others hardly bear the authority of D. The reading of D at John 1:3/4 must be reckoned with—whatever it is.

Apart from a review of the history of the problem, the ambiguity of D on John 1:3/4 is suitably reflected in the following.

(1) The D reading with two stops clearly is not an invention of the modern imagination. It has long been included in the *critici apparatus* of various editions of the Greek New Testament, and, anyway, is not unique in the manuscript tradition.

(2) Westcott examined the manuscript prior to the publication of his commentary on John and declared emphatically that no dot followed ὃ γέγονεν. His full statement is:

> A careful and repeated examination of D satisfies me completely that this MS. has no stop after γέγονεν. There is a slight flaw in the vellum which extends towards γέγονεν from the top of the following ε, of which the upper boundary is above the level of the writing, but this is certainly not the vestige of a stop. The stops are below the level of the writing. And again, there is no increased space between γέγονεν and ἐν such as is found where a stop occurs, as between οὐδέν and ὅ. On holding the leaf to the light, the point of a C falls within the flaw and gives the semblance of a stop.[66]

(3) Nestle cites D as punctuating only before ὃ γέγονεν through all twenty-six editions (1898-1979).

(4) The first edition of the United Bible Societies' *Greek New Testament* (1966) suddenly cites D as giving a dot once again before and after.

(5) Aland, who was the chief editor of the UBS edition and who also examined the manuscript, calls that a mistake. Whether Aland meant that it was a clerical error or that he disagrees with the editorial committee's judgment one cannot tell for certain, but his statement would appear to favor the latter inasmuch as he indicts also Scrivener's edition for the same error: "Scrivener und Greek New Testament sind mit ihren Angaben im

---

[65] Aland perhaps overstates the matter with his claim that "den Zeilenbruch als solches anzusehen, dürfte nicht möglich sein" ("Eine Untersuchung zu Joh. 1:3-4," p. 189).

[66] Westcott, *The Gospel according to St. John*, p. 29, n. 1.

Unrecht."[67] In any event, the UBS' subsequent editions cite D as punctuating only before ὃ γέγονεν.

But the initial UBS citation of D as punctuating both before and after
is not to be lightly passed off, for I am persuaded on the basis of my own
firsthand examination of D in Cambridge on August 28, 1971, that both
Westcott and Aland missed something. It is true that a *prima facie* observation, and even a more careful one, suggests immediately that there is only
one punctuation mark involved in the passage, a bold, well-spaced
elevated dot preceding ὃ γέγονεν. There is indeed what at first appears to
be an elevated smudge between ὃ γέγονεν and ἐν but one is able quickly
to recognize this as the flaw that Westcott spoke of. Viewing the passage
at the time under ultraviolet light only revealed that "something is going
on" between the two words, but no dot was emphatically resolved. However, a more careful scrutiny through a magnifying glass and a tilting of
the leaf toward the sunlight reveals directly below the Westcott flaw, just
above the faint line that runs through the middle of the letters used by
the scribe as a guide, though not above the upper level of the letters, what
decidedly appears to be the remnant of a dot. It is small, it is extremely
pale, it is wedged in between the two words without appropriate space,
but it is there. (This judgment is confirmed by Mr. A. E. B. Owen, chief
paleographer at the Cambridge University Library, who examined the
manuscript with me. It is further confirmed by more leisurely examination of ultraviolet and infrared photographs of the passage.)

If, then, there is a dot at the disputed place, the question becomes:
How did it get there, how are we to account for this early (perhaps
earliest?) and enigmatic punctuation before *and* after ὃ γέγονεν? One must
at this point necessarily indulge in some measure of speculation, and I
suggest the following merely as the explanation that commends itself as
best accounting for all the facts:

(1) The original reading punctuated before ὃ γέγονεν only.

(2) A later editor or owner of the manuscript, familiar with the alternate reading which punctuated only after ὃ γέγονεν, cautiously inserted
a second dot after γέγονεν either in the interest of thereby building support for the (by then) theologically more desirable reading, or simply for
the purpose of conveniently reminding the reader of this interesting and
important variation in the text, or for the purpose of bringing this manuscript into harmony with several late manuscripts which (beginning in the
8th century?) had begun to adopt the double punctuation (which
naturally presupposes that the later double-punctuation was not itself
dependent upon D). Of course, if one could believe in the originality of

---

[67] Aland, "Eine Untersuchung zu Joh. 1:3-4," p. 188, n. 18.

D's double-punctuation, then this might (in view of the difficulty of accounting for late but difficult readings) hold some interesting implications for the general relation of D to these later manuscripts.

(3) The second dot, whenever penned, was so cautiously and lightly penned as almost to disappear over the years, or was deliberately erased or scraped out (if one uses the imagination, one can perceive an ever-so-slight concavity in the vellum where the dot stood) by a still later party who, recognizing what had occurred, and possessing a greater sensitivity to the use and abuse of manuscripts, sought to restore what was obviously the original version. It should be observed that here we have an instance where the *lectio difficilior* principle works exactly in reverse, namely, when there is no possible way of accounting for an original reading which makes no sense whatever, or is at least completely ambiguous (an elevated dot both before and after ὃ γέγονεν), and it is possible to account for such a reading on the hypothesis of a correction or aid.

If there is indeed a dot, or the remnant of a dot, in D following ὃ γέγονεν, then the *apparatus* of the UBS's edition is correct in citing D as punctuating before and after. On the other hand, if the second punctuation is to be accounted for somewhat along the lines as I have suggested, then the UBS edition is wrong in not distinguishing between first- and second-hand readings in this instance as it does in others. In fact, whereas with respect to the reading of D the United Bible Societies' *criticus apparatus* should but does not distinguish between the original and corrected versions, it does draw this distinction in the case of the reading of P[75], where it probably should not. Which brings us, finally, to:

(iii)[68] We saw earlier that in 1880 Westcott declared that a stronger attestation than we have for *Reading II* could scarcely be hoped for.[69] But even this has turned out to be an understatement, for the textual evidence has swung even more decisively in favor of *Reading II*. Four Greek papyri containing parts of the New Testament were published by the Bodmer Library of Geneva beginning in the mid-1950s. Of these, P[66] and P[75] contain portions of John, including the passage under consideration.[70]

P[66], which dates from about 200 (perhaps even earlier),[71] is punc-

---

[68] The following is adapted with minor editing from my article, "P[66] and P[75] on John 1:3/4," *TZ*, 41 (1985), pp. 440ff.

[69] Westcott, *The Gospel according to St. John*, p. 4.

[70] Victor Martin (ed.), *Papyrus Bodmer II: Évangile de Jean, chap. 1-14* (Cologny-Geneva: Bibliotheca Bodmeriana, 1958), revised ed. by Victor Martin and J. W. B. Barns (1962); Victor Martin and Rodolphe Kasser (eds.), *Papyrus Bodmer XIV-XV: Évangile de Luc, chap. 3-24, Évangile de Jean, chap. 1-15* (Cologny-Geneva: Bibliotheca Bodmeriana, 1961). See Schnackenburg's summarizing discussion and bibliographical notes on the significance of P[66] and P[75]: *Das Johannesevangelium*, I, pp. 156ff.

[71] Herbert Hunger argues for an earlier dating, even possibly the first half of the second century ("Zur Datierung des Papyrus Bodmer II (P[66])," *Anzeiger der österreichischen Akademie der Wissenschaften*, phil.-hist. Kl., 4 (1966), pp. 12ff.).

tuated only sporadically and, unfortunately, not at all at vss. 3-4. It may,
nonetheless, bear some evidence for the reading of the passage. Barrett,
in his "preliminary reconaissance" of P⁶⁶, speculates that the missing ἐν
of vs. 4a of P⁶⁶ is due to an error of haplography and that the MS. thus
"inclines slightly" to *Reading I*.⁷² But one may draw from the
haplographic omission of ἐν a different conclusion: The haplography itself
is most easily explained by an unbroken continuity between the words
γέγονεν ἐν, that is, with no stop after ὃ γέγονεν. Though this latter
possibility militates against the original P⁶⁶ = *Reading I*, in itself it is not
of course evidence for the original P⁶⁶ = *Reading II* either, for the fact
remains that no punctuation concludes οὐδέν (which P⁶⁶ reads in the
place of οὐδὲ ἕν). It may, however, be evidence that the copyist at least
understood the passage according to *Reading II*. This view of the matter
gains credibility in light of the number of scholars who favor it, including
de la Potterie, Massaux, Vawter, Schnackenburg, and Aland.⁷³ Perhaps
less forceful is the suggestion of Teeple and Walker that the original
P⁶⁶ = *Reading I* on the grounds that a stop may have once stood in the
extra space preceding ὃ γέγονεν though disappearing over a period of
time.⁷⁴ Aland is rightfully skeptical about the dot-disappeared, calling
attention to a similar interval one line below between τὸ and φῶς.⁷⁵ Still,
when all these considerations are added up they yield the suggestion that
P⁶⁶ "inclines slightly" not to *Reading I* but to *Reading II*. In any event, the
relevance of P⁶⁶ for the reading of John 1:3/4 has now been over-
shadowed by the text of P⁷⁵.

The importance of the discovery of P⁷⁵ is reflected by Metzger who
emphasizes the "effect of the discovery of P⁷⁵ on textual theory" and
declares that "the textual significance of this newly acquired witness is hard
to over-estimate."⁷⁶ P⁷⁵ is a Vaticanus-type text dating from the end of
the second century.⁷⁷ It is a carefully executed manuscript,⁷⁸ and its

⁷² C. K. Barrett, "Papyrus Bodmer II: A Preliminary Report," *ET*, 68 (1956-57), p. 175.
⁷³ I. de la Potterie, "Een nieuwe papyrus van het vierde Evangelie, Papyrus Bodmer II," *Bijdragen*, 18 (1957), p. 122; Édouard Massaux, "Le Papyrus Bodmer II (P⁶⁶) et la Critique Néotestamentaire," in *Sacra Pagina: Miscellanea Biblica Congressus Internationalis Catholici de re Biblica*, (Gembloux: J. Duculof, 1959), I, pp. 203f.; Bruce Vawter, "What Came to Be in Him Was Life (Jn. 1:3b-4a)," p. 401 and n. 3; Schnackenburg, *Das Johannesevangelium*, I, p. 215f. and n. 5; Aland, "Eine Untersuchung zu Joh. 1:3-4," p. 189, n. 19.
⁷⁴ H. M. Teeple and F. A. Walker, "Notes on the Plates in Papyrus Bodmer II," *JBL*, 78 (1959), p. 149.
⁷⁵ Aland, "Eine Untersuchung zu Joh. 1:3-4," p. 189, n. 19.
⁷⁶ Bruce M. Metzger, *Historical and Literary Studies* (Leiden: Brill, 1968), p. 152, and "The Bodmer Papyrus of Luke and John," *ET*, 73 (1961-62), p. 202.
⁷⁷ The Vaticanus character of P⁷⁵ was first indicated by Victor Martin and Rodolphe Kasser, *Papyrus Bodmer XIV-XV*, p. 29. On the relation of P⁷⁵ to Vaticanus, see also Calvin L. Porter, "Papyrus Bodmer XV (P⁷⁵) and the Text of Codex Vaticanus," *JBL*, 81 (1962),

physical condition is such that scarcely a letter has been challenged, though it appears once to have fallen into the hands of doodlers, including a child who, using it as a copy book (!), imperfectly reproduced the first words of one of the leaves.

As it bears specifically on our question, P[75] clearly shows an elevated dot—admittedly a *hypostigme* rather than a *teleia stigme*, indicating a minor pause—before ὅ γέγονεν and no punctuation after it, that is, *Reading II*. The *criticus apparatus* of the UBS *Greek New Testament* cites the original hand of P[75] as giving no punctuation at all and a corrected version of P[75] as giving *Reading II*. But this may be misleading. The same is true of Metzger's comment in his *Textual Commentary on the Greek New Testament*: "Should the words ὅ γέγονεν be joined with what goes before or with what follows? The oldest MSS. (P[66], P[75]*, ℵ, A, B) have no punctuation here. . . ."[79] It requires considerable self-assurance on the part of these scholars to judge the punctuation of P[75] at this point to be the work of a later corrector. An examination of the photographic plate of this passage does reveal a "crowding," but this is not unusual; the plates of John 3 (chosen at random) reveal a similar crowding at vss. 4, 6-7, 8-9, 17, and 19; and at any rate there is no reason to doubt that such additions (if they were additions) were made on the spot by the scribe himself. On this last point we concur with Aland that though there is not here as great an interval between the words as would be expected,

---

pp. 363ff., in which, among other things, he provides a complete collation of the 205 variations (omitting orthographic variations, scribal errors, etc.) of B from P[75]. One should note also Kenneth Willis Clark's discussion, "The Text of the Gospel of John in Third-Century Egypt," *NT*, 5 (1962), pp. 17ff., especially his comments on p. 24:

. . . there is a notable affinity between the third-century P[75] and the fourth-century Codex Vaticanus, whose textual relationship is closer than that of any other pair among the earliest witnesses.

. . . it is our judgment that P[75] appears to have the best textual character in the third century; and that it is this text of P[75] that bears most closely upon the textual character of Codex Vaticanus in the fourth century. Although this cannot be considered to be the unique orthodox text, it does appear that the textual descent from P[75] to Vaticanus contains the more consistent and significant textual quality. We conclude therefore that the key to the true textual history is P[75], our newest available witness for the text of the Gospel of John in third-century Egypt.

[78] For an analysis of the scribal integrity of P[75], see Ernest C. Colwell, "Methods in Evaluating Scribal Habits: A Study of P[45], P[66], P[75]," in *Studies in Methodology in Textual Criticism of the New Testament* (Grand Rapids, Mich.: Eerdmans, 1969), pp. 106ff. Colwell demonstrates that the scribe of P[75] copied his MS. letter by letter, and concludes that "in P[75] the text that is produced can be explained in all its variants as the result of a single force, namely the disciplined scribe who writes with the intention of being careful and accurate" (p. 117). On the other hand, Metzger is certainly correct in seeing in Luke 11:31, 17:14, and John 5:5 additions made by a different hand ("The Bodmer Papyrus of Luke and John," p. 202).

[79] Bruce Metzger, *A Textual Commentary on the Greek New Testament* (London: United Bible Societies, 1971), p. 195.

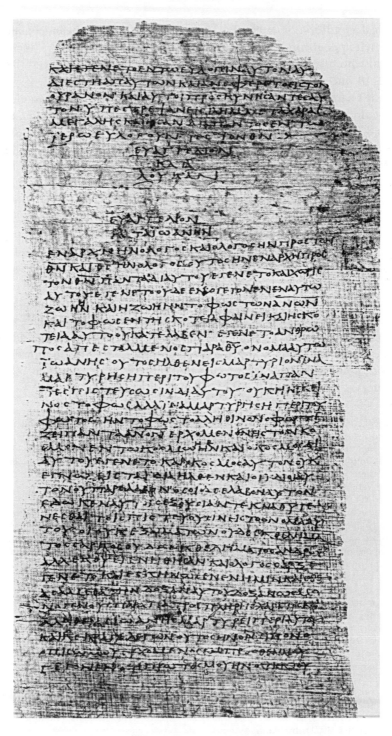

P⁷⁵, Luke 24:51—John 1:1-16

wahrscheinlich ist der Punkt bei der an die Niederschrift anschliessend Durchsicht und Korrektur zugesetzt worden, mindestens ist hier dieselbe Feder am Werke gewesen, der Punkt unterscheidet sich in seinem Character nicht von den anderen.[80]

Thus also V. Martin:

D'une manière générale, on peut dire que les fautes qui subsistent sont relativement peu nombreuses. Quant aux corrections, certaines d'entre elles, en tout cas, ont dû être faites de suite, au cours de la transcription, par le copiste lui-même. . . . Une revision méthodique du texte n'est cependant guère probable en présence des imperfections qui subsistent.[81]

And Colwell: "There is no evidence of revision of his work by anyone else, or in fact of any real revision, or check."[82]

P[75] is, therefore, possibly our earliest witness to John 1:3/4, certainly our earliest punctuated witness, and it gives *Reading II*. It also gives, as should be emphasized, the *lectio difficilior*. Whether it is possible to draw any good theological sense out of this reading is, of course, the further question.

With respect to the all-important witness of the punctuated MS. P[75] (as well as later ones), it could be countered that it is nevertheless not possible to know the punctuation of the original document, not even if we possessed it. Our earliest manuscripts contained no accentuation, no breaks between words, no breaks between sentences, and very little punctuation, which was introduced only toward the end of the second century. The autograph thus contained no punctuation at all. Unless, then, one believes that all punctuation is given by inspiration of God, the earliest punctuation may have been—indeed must have been—a matter of interpretation. For this reason even the earliest punctuation holds no strictly textual authority. On the other hand, it does hold exegetical and historical authority. That is, it holds the same kind of interpretation-authority as the writings of the Fathers. Metzger's observation about the relevance of patristic evidence would seem to apply with equal force to the punctuation of MSS.: It may possibly be of assistance in ascertaining the original text of the New Testament, but it always elucidates the history of the transmission of varying forms of that text.[83] As with the Fathers, manuscript-punctuation reflects an understanding—in the case of P[75] an early understanding—of a passage, and not just someone's or anyone's

---

[80] Aland, "Eine Untersuchung zu Joh. 1:3-4," p. 189.
[81] Martin and Kasser, *Papyrus Bodmer XIV-XV*, p. 24.
[82] Colwell, "Methods in Evaluating Scribal Habits," p. 117.
[83] Cf. Bruce M. Metzger, "Patristic Evidence and the Textual Criticism of the New Testament," *NTS*, 18 (1971-72), pp. 397ff..

understanding, but presumably a traditional or community understanding. In this latter respect, manuscript-punctuation may for that
matter hold even more authority than the Fathers inasmuch as the
copyists even less than the Fathers had any theological axes to grind.

In the meantime, there is yet another textual consideration which may
bear on the punctuation of John 1:3/4. In relationship to the question of
ὃ γέγονεν, the two instances of ἦν which follow it must be considered: ὃ
γέγονεν ἐν αὐτῷ ζωὴ ἦν, καὶ ἡ ζωὴ ἦν τὸ φῶς τῶν ἀνθρώπων. What is relevant
here is that there is some important textual evidence for ἐστίν in place of
the ἦν of the first clause, and likewise some evidence even for the ἦν of
the second clause, though this is almost nil.

It is, in fact, almost certain on the basis of the textual evidence (as well
as another consideration mentioned below) that the original reading in
the first clause was not ἐστίν but ἦν, which, after all, is the reading supported by P⁶⁶, P⁷⁵, A, B, C, the Vulgate, and a host of other MSS., Versions, and Fathers.[84] But if we assume that the original text read ἦν, then
it may be argued that the ἦν could have easily become ἐστίν on the
gramatically and/or theologically inspired belief that since ὃ γέγονεν
belonged to vs. 4 it therefore required a present tense in the main clause.
This is supported by the coincidence of the authorities for *Reading II* and
the authorities for ἐστίν, and, in any case, there is no other likely reason
for ἦν to have become ἐστίν—certainly the ἐστίν can more easily be
explained in connection with the preceding perfect γέγονεν than in connection with the following imperfect ἦν. Thus ἐστίν is excluded as the
original reading, but only because ὃ γέγονεν is taken with vs. 4, that is,
Reading II. Further, א (or an even earlier MS. from which it was copied),
which gives no punctuation but does give ἐστίν, becomes a sort of left-
handed witness (and a very strong one) for *Reading II*; that is, the bare
fact of an ἐστίν in the first clause suggests an *understanding* of the text
according to *Reading II*.

In place of the ἦν in the first clause, ἐστίν is given in (or implied by) א,
D, the Old Latin, the Old Syriac Curetonianus, the Sahidic and
Fayyumic Coptic, most Fathers, and most Gnostics. The evidence for
ἐστίν is thus not strong as compared to the evidence for ἦν (see above).

---

[84] *Contra* Boismard who regards the originality of the present tense ἐστίν as conclusive
from the point of view of the manuscript evidence alone (*Le Prologue de Saint Jean*, pp. 24f.).
Indeed, he holds out, rather exceptionally, for a present tense ἐστίν in *both* instances in
vs. 4. But his treatment of the textual problem here is implausible. He opts for the first
ἐστίν on the basis of what is in fact relatively weak MS. evidence, and then posits the
second ἐστίν, which rests on even weaker MS. evidence, simply because it "doit être au
même temps que le premier" (p. 25). Perhaps the evidence of P⁶⁶ and P⁷⁵, published
subsequently to his work on the Prologue, would have caused him to modify his view. But
perhaps not. He also opts for the singular ὅς at vs. 13!

Nonetheless, if we were to grant the originality of ἐστίν what would follow for our problem? A present tense ἐστίν in the first clause would more naturally follow the perfect γέγονεν than the perfect γέγονεν would follow the previous aorist ἐγένετο. If, then, the original did read ἐστίν (and was changed to ἦν presumably in order to bring it into harmony with the virtually undisputed ἦν of the second clause), we would take it as evidence that ὃ γέγονεν was originally construed with vs. 4, that is, *Reading II*. On the other hand, if the argument for an original present-tense ἐστίν here cannot be made conclusive (which it hardly can), then nothing at all follows for the placing of ὃ γέγονεν since it is no more problematic for it to be construed with an aorist of a main clause preceding it than with an imperfect of a main clause following it.

It must be mentioned, though, that some have extended this very reasoning as grounds against, rather than for, *Reading II*. For example, Zahn argued precisely as we have done above (ἦν became ἐστίν because ὃ γέγονεν was understood with vs. 4) but for the purpose of demonstrating the originality of *Reading I*: The change from ζωὴ ἦν to ζωὴ ἐστίν is to be explained as a textual corruption which developed under the influence of *Reading II*; but whereas, according to Zahn, the perfect γέγονεν, on *Reading II*, requires the present ἐστίν, the no-doubt original ἦν argues for taking ὃ γέγονεν with vs. 3, *Reading I*.[85]

However, Zahn surely overplays his hand when he announces,

> . . . die dadurch hergestellte Verbindung von ὃ γέγονεν ἐν αὐτῷ ζωὴ ἦν zu einem neuen selbständigen Satz ist weder sprachlich noch sachlich zu rechtfertigen. . . . in der Tat passt das Imperf. ἦν nicht in einen Nachsatz, dessen Subjekt der Vordersatz ὃ γέγονεν bildet. . . . Es musste entweder gesagt sein ὃ ἐγεγόνει (allenfalls auch ἐγένετο) . . . ζωὴ ἦν, oder ὃ γέγονεν . . . ζωή ἐστιν.[86]

As for the *sprachlich* question, we grant that the perfect followed by the imperfect results in a linguistic infelicity (which indeed explains the origin of the ἐστίν), but we do not grant that it is impossible, nor, in any case, that it yields a greater infelicity than the alternative of taking the perfect with the preceding οὐδὲ ἕν. It has already been observed, in our earlier discussion of the linguistic considerations, that in the latter case (taking ὃ γέγονεν with the preceding οὐδὲ ἕν) more natural Greek would give οὐδὲ ἓν ὧν γέγονεν.[87] And, at any rate, the copyists of other witnesses

---

[85] Zahn, *Das Evangelium des Johannes*, pp. 52f.

[86] Zahn, *Das Evangelium des Johannes*, pp. 52f. Note also Bernhard Weiss' comment that "das Perf. γέγονεν, welches einen Fortbestand bezeichnet, nicht ἦν, sonder ἐστίν nach ζωή logisch erfordert haben würde" (*Das Evangelium des Johannes: Kritischer und exegetischer Kommentar* (Göttingen: Vandenhoeck & Ruprecht, 1880), p. 41).

[87] So, we may recall, Bultmann, *Das Evangelium des Johannes*, p. 21, n. 2, and Schnackenburg, *Das Johannesevangelium*, I, p. 216.

which clearly construe ὃ γέγονεν with the imperfect ἦν knew Greek too but apparently did not stumble over this construction nor were seized by an irresistible impulse to improve upon it. As for the *sachlich* problem, this is a problem only on a certain interpretation of ὃ γέγονεν, and thus it must be reserved until one has had a chance to consider the meaning of ὃ γέγονεν, and this will take us far into Chapter II of our study.

Thus far we have left aside the problem of the concluding οὐδέν or οὐδὲ ἕν of vs. 3, but now this too must finally be addressed. Actually there can be little question from a purely textcritical standpoint about the correctness of the reading οὐδὲ ἕν: οὐδέν is given in P⁶⁶, ℵ*, D, a few Fathers, some miniscules, and some Gnostics, but οὐδὲ ἕν is supported by virtually all other witnesses. As it bears on our punctuation-problem, Zahn took the originality of οὐδὲ ἕν as evidence for *Reading I*, for the later οὐδέν must have been substituted for οὐδὲ ἕν which would have become an intolerable conclusion of vs. 3 when ὃ γέγονεν was eventually assimilated to vs. 4 (*Reading II*).[88] But, as we said in an earlier discussion, there is nothing implausible about a concluding οὐδὲ ἕν; it was in fact a common Greek construction. It occurs also at the end of a clause at 3:27 (according to the best witnesses), and the otherwise resulting οὐδὲ ἓν ὃ γέγονεν would be stylistically anticlimactic. Haenchen, quite to the contrary of Zahn, believes that though the emphatic οὐδὲ ἕν is more suitable for the end of the sentence, it reflects the tendency in MSS. to substitute οὐδὲ ἕν for the older οὐδέν.[89]

The fact is that the textual problem of οὐδὲ ἕν/οὐδέν is probably irrelevant for the decision between *Reading I* and *Reading II* inasmuch as either οὐδὲ ἕν or οὐδέν favors ever so slightly *Reading II*. Again reminiscent of discussions above: John had a penchant for ending sentences or clauses with οὐδέν, οὐδένα, etc., and a concluding οὐδὲ ἕν would seem to reflect the same, though more emphatic, stylistic stamp; either an οὐδὲ ἕν or an οὐδέν at the end of vs. 1:3 would, therefore, be consistent with this Johannine practice, and would suggest, at least, *Reading II*. Furthermore, as we saw earlier, we must reckon with the question whether either an οὐδὲ ἕν or an οὐδέν would on *Reading I* normally be followed by ὃ γέγονεν rather than ὧν γέγονεν in case of οὐδὲ ἕν or ὅ τι γέγονεν in the case of οὐδέν.

To this point we have been considering linguistic and textual-critical evidence for the placing of ὃ γέγονεν as the conclusion of John 1:3 (that is, *Reading I*) or the beginning of 1:4 (*Reading II*). We may mention, finally, that some have been driven by the difficulty of this passage to assume a

[88] Zahn, *Das Evangelium des Johannes*, p. 53.
[89] Haenchen, "Probleme des johanneischen 'Prologs'", p. 316, n. 51.

corruption of the text and the impossibility of recovering the original version. A good example of this is Schwartz:

> Es hilft kein Drehen und Wenden: hier hat ein Überarbeiter einem überlieferten Wortlaut einen neuen Sinn aufzwingen wollen, in dem er ihn teilweise änderte und teilweise stehen liess, und es ist aussichtslos das Ursprüngliche wiedergewinnen zu wollen. Nur unsicher lässt sich ahnen, was der Überarbeiter meinte, da er seine eigenen Worte mit fremden vermischt hat.[90]

Such a desperate hypothesis is unnecessary. We will see in the next chapter that the desperation grows out of a failure to reckon with an altogether different—and plausible—interpretation of ὃ γέγονεν than has been usually considered. Still more extreme is the view which excises ὃ γέγονεν altogether, explaining it as an interpolation. This is the view of Hirsch who believed the ὃ γέγονεν was intruded into the text by a redactor (sometime between 130 and 140) who sought therewith to counter the possible gnostic employment of the text as teaching the origin of Chaos or "das Nichts": "All things came into being through him, and apart from him came into being Nothing."[91] Hirsch's hypothesis hardly inspires confidence. Aside from the fact that there is no textual evidence whatsoever for the omission of ὃ γέγονεν, surely a more concrete scenario must be provided for its origin. Furthermore, as Aland points out, Hirsch's whole theory about the redaction during 130-140 is immediately thrown into doubt inasmuch as Hirsch also argued in 1936 that John 18:32 was certainly the contribution of the redactor,[92] whereas it is contained in the MS. scrap P[52] found subsequently in Egypt and dated about 125.[93]

The evidence, then, for the punctuation of John 1:3/4 may be developed along the above lines. Feuillet is an example of those who think that no decision about *Reading I* vs. *Reading II* can be made on the basis of such considerations—linguistic and textual evidence are both indecisive.[94] Our impression is different. Attempts to justify *Reading I* or *Reading II* on linguistic grounds tend to cancel themselves out, though we find in such considerations a balance of evidence in favor of *Reading II*. As for textual evidence, we have seen that the weight of the punctuated authorities supports *Reading II*. More specifically, we have emphasized the special significance of the early Fathers as evidence for *Reading II*, the probable authority of D for *Reading II*, and the certain relevance of P[75], one

---

[90] Eduard Schwartz, "Aporien im vierten Evangelium, IV," *Nachrichten von der königlichen Gesellschaft der Wissenschaften zu Göttingen*, phil.-hist. Kl. (1908), p. 535. Cf. also Bauer, *Das Johannesevangelium*, p. 11.

[91] Emanuel Hirsch, *Studien zum vierten Evangelium* (Tübingen: Mohr, 1936), p. 44.

[92] Hirsch, *Studien zum vierten Evangelium*, p. 121.

[93] Aland, "Eine Untersuchung zu Joh. 1:3-4," p. 177, n. 6.

[94] Feuillet, *Le Prologue du Quatrième Évangile*, pp. 38f.

of the earliest and best MS. witnesses. We further suggested how the subsequent problem in vs. 4 of the ἦν-become-ἐστίν in some MSS. (sometimes twice) may be construed as evidence for *Reading II*. It has been apparent throughout that *Reading II* is the *lectio difficilior*, though we have reserved full emphasis and exploration of this for Chapter II.

All of the evidence considered above, taken cumulatively, suggests emphatically that the earliest interpretations took ὃ γέγονεν with vs. 4, and that, therefore, *Reading II* has the strongest claim to originality.

CHAPTER TWO

THE INTERPRETATION

On the basis of the textual considerations raised in Chapter I we have concluded that John 1:4a according to *Reading II*, which joins ὅ γέγονεν with what follows (ὅ γέγονεν ἐν αὐτῷ ζωὴ ἦν), is probably original. But it is one thing to conclude that *Reading II* is original and quite another to make good sense of it. We come, then, to the *crux interpretum*.

It has been apparent throughout that *Reading II* is the *lectio difficilior*, and the *difficultas* here should not be underestimated. Metzger summarizes the problem when he calls *Reading II* "intolerably clumsy and opaque."[1] So did Bauer a long time ago with his charge that *Reading II* makes no sense at all, not in antiquity nor for us, not within the Church nor outside it.[2] Schnackenburg rejects *Reading II* because "bereitet die Verbindung . . . grosse Schwierigkeiten."[3] According to Morris, *Reading II* "gives us an exceedingly complicated expression in v. 4. I am not sure that those who adopt this view really face the difficulties."[4] To be sure, the problem of making sense of *Reading II* is recognized by virtually everyone. *Lectiones difficiliores* come in two (sometimes overlapping) varieties: Those readings that are more difficult because they involve some linguistic or grammatical problem, and those that are more difficult because they give rise to some theological problem. *Reading II-A* is grammatically coherent, and even though *Reading II-B* is anacoluthic we have noted that such constructions are not uncommon in John. The problem concerns not the grammar of the phrase but its meaning. The question now before us is: Can we assign to *Reading II* any good theological and Johannine sense?

The Lectio Difficilior *and the Origins of* Reading I

It is very important now to note that the problem, the *difficultas*, in *Reading II* arises when ὅ γέγονεν is thought to refer in some way to something *created*, or, more specifically, when it is regarded as a continuation, restatement, or extension of the πάντα (= the created world) in vs. 3. It was, surely, some such interpretation of *Reading II* which already in anti-

---

[1] Metzger, *A Textual Commentary on the Greek New Testament*, p. 196, n. 2.
[2] Bauer, *Das Johannesevangelium*, p. 11.
[3] Schnackenburg, *Das Johannesevangelium*, I, p. 216.
[4] Morris, *The Gospel according to John*, p. 82.

quity was perceived as heretical and which thus inspired the fourth century abandonment of the now heretical-sounding *Reading II* and the
introduction of the more innocuous *Reading I*.

Whether the origin and motivation of *Reading I* may be identified more
precisely than this is a difficult question. That it was at one time
employed as a polemic against the Arians is clear from St. Ambrose who,
in his commentary on the Psalms, addresses directly the new reading
which joins ὃ γέγονεν with vs. 3, that is *Reading I*:

> Alexandrini quidem et Aegyptii legunt: "Omnia per ipsum facta sunt, et
> sine ipso factum est nihil quod factum est"; et interposita distinctione subi-
> ciunt: "In ipso vita est." Salva sit fidelibus illa distinctio: ego non vereor
> legere: "Quod Factum est in ipso vita est"; et nihil habet quod teneat
> Arianus, quia non illius venena considero, sed lectionis sacrae con-
> suetudinem recognosco. Non enim dixit: "Factum est Verbum ante omne
> principium." Non dixit: "Factum est Verbum"; sed si quod dixerit audire
> desideras: "Verbum," inquit, "Erat apud Deum." Erat apud Deum, quod
> cum ipso operabatur, cum ipso dominabatur. Non dixit: "Factum est Ver-
> bum," sed dixit: "Deus erat Verbum"; Deus autem non factura, sed factor
> est et creator. Aperi aures, et audi: "Omnia per ipsum facta sunt, et sine
> ipso factum est nihil." Discis esse Filium, in quo divinitatis est plenitudo?
> Aperi aures adhuc paululum, et audi dicentem: "Quod factum est in ipso,
> vita est." "In ipso," inquit, "factum est"; non "Dei Verbum factum est." Aut
> si hoc movet te ad calumniam, quia dixit: "In ipso factum est," numquid
> et Deo Patri calumnaris, quia Dei Filius dixit: "Qui autem facit veritatem,
> venit ad lucem ut manifestentur opera eius, quia in Deo sunt facta?" Aut
> quia David dixit: "Confitebor tibi, Domine, quoniam exaudisti me, et
> factus es mihi in salutem"; hoc est, conversus es mihi in salutem, operatus
> es mihi ad salutem? Possem aliis uti, sed nolo mihi credas; ne putes
> argumenta esse ingenii, non testimonia veritatis.[5]

Thus Ambrose criticizes the new reading (*Reading I*) which he regards as
having been conceived in the interest of disarming the Arians who, on the
basis of the older *Reading II*, taught that the Son himself was a created
being, had undergone changes, and was therefore not equal to the
Father.[6] He regards *Reading I* as the more "safe" for the faithful, but has
himself no problem with *Reading II*: The Arians can make no legitimate
use of this line, for its immediate context states unequivocally that the
Logos *was* God, and the line itself speaks of what was made *in* him.

It is not clear who the Alexandrians and Egyptians mentioned by
Ambrose were, but some (for example, Zahn, Hoskyns/Davey, and

---

[5] St. Ambrose, *In Psalmum*, XXXVI, 35 (*PL*, 14, 1030ff.) Cf. the somewhat later *De Fide*, III, 41ff. (*PL*, 16, 622f.).

[6] Of course, the Arians who, like most others, identified the Johannine Logos with the Old Testament Wisdom, made much of the createdness of Wisdom as asserted, for example, in Prov. 8:22.

Boismard[7]) have cited Alexander, Bishop of Alexandria (d. 328), as the first to employ *Reading I*. The evidence for this is Theodoret who in his *Historia Ecclesiastica* preserves a passage from Alexander's *Epistola* containing a citation of John 1:1-3 in the form of *Reading I*.[8] But Alexander's role in this has now been thrown into doubt by both Mehlmann and Aland who have argued that our text of Theodoret is at this point highly suspect. Theodoret quotes Alexander as concluding vs. 3 with ὃ γέγονεν (= *Reading I*) according to the eleventh century Codex Vaticanus 628 and the 13th century Marcianus 344. But all other codices, most of them older, omit the ὃ γέγονεν (= *Reading II*), and in this respect L. Parmentier's critical edition of Theodoret, published already in 1911, is most important in supporting *Reading II* as the actual reading employed by Alexander in his *Epistola*. As for the Vaticanus and Marciannus texts, which include ὃ γέγονεν with vs. 3 (= *Reading I*), this very likely simply reflects the common reading of John 1:1-3 which had established itself long before the time of these codices and was considered standard by the copyists.[9]

Mehlmann himself, followed by Schnackenburg, rejects the anti-Arian origin of *Reading I* on the grounds that *Reading I* is at least as old as Adamantius' dialogue *De Recta in Deum Fide*, "a witness which," says Mehlmann, "seems to my knowledge to have escaped the commentators' attention but might well take over the place of the first *known* witness to that reading" (i.e. *Reading I*).[10] Here (*PG*, 11, 1829), the Greek text of John 1:3 is quoted and ὃ γέγονεν is taken with vs. 3 (= *Reading I*). And if, as Mehlmann accepts in agreement with many others, the dialogue originated in Syria prior to 311, then *Reading I* could hardly have originated at Alexandria as a polemic against Arius who launched his controversy with Alexander about 320. It originated, Mehlmann believes, in a quite different context:

---

[7] Zahn, *Das Evangelium des Johannes*, p. 710; Edwyn Clement Hoskyns, *The Fourth Gospel*, ed. Francis Noel Davey, second ed. (London: Faber, 1947), p. 142; Boismard, *Le Prologue de Saint Jean*, p. 27. Cf. Zahn who speaks of "die ungesuchte Weise, wie sie [i.e. *Reading I*] schon im ersten Anfang des Streites von Alexander vorgebracht wird" (p. 711).

[8] Theodoret, *Historia Ecclesiastica*, I, 4 (*PG*, 82, 893).

[9] J. Mehlmann, "A Note on John 1:3," *ET*, 67 (1955-56), pp. 340f.; Aland, "Eine Untersuchung zu Joh. 1:3-4," pp. 196f. Aland observes that it is a testimony to the tenacity of "tradition" that, even after the publication of Parmentier's edition of Theodoret, Zahn continued in subsequent editions of his commentary to hold his initial representation of the matter, and many commentators after him (p. 197). Note also Aland's criticism of Zahn's uncritical use of the material even before Parmentier's edition (p. 196, n. 24).

[10] Mehlmann, "A Note on John 1:3," p. 340. Cf. Schnackenburg, *Das Johannesevangelium*, I, p. 216 (though, as we have seen, Schnackenburg actually accepts the originality of *Reading I*). Aland ("Eine Untersuchung zu Joh. 1:3-4," p. 183) credits Schnackenburg for the dethroning of Alexander as the earliest attestation of *Reading I*, but Schnackenburg himself cites Mehlmann for the discovery of the Adamantius passage (*Das Johannesevangelium*, p. 216, n. 1).

> The Dialogue would then not only be prior to Arius and to St. Alexander's Letter, as well as alien to their country, but it deals furthermore with quite another set of heretics, namely the followers of Marcion, Bardesanes and Valentinus.[11]

As Mehlmann notes, it was not only the Arians but pre-Arian heretics too who followed consistently *Reading II* and made much mileage out of it. Augustine, in his commentary on John, warns us explicitly not to interpret the text of John 1:3/4a (*Reading II*) as do that "sordidissima secta Manichaeorum," who on the basis of it claim that a stone has life and a wall has a soul.[12] It is certain too, as we know from Irenaeus, Clement of Alexandria, and others, that the Valentinians employed *Reading II* in a Gnostic manner, construing ὃ γέγονεν ἐν αὐτῷ as the Aeon ζωή, a syzygy of the Logos.[13] And it would be possible for other Gnostics, such as Ptolemaeus, to find in *Reading II* Johannine support for their doctrine of the origin of the Ogdoad.[14] And Heracleon employed *Reading II* as a proof-text for the special life imparted to the Pneumatomachi: ἐν αὐτῷ is a generic reference to those human beings who are pneumatic.[15] We cite these only as a few examples of the wide use of *Reading II* by the Gnostics.[16]

But that *Reading I* arose as a counter-attack to the pre-Arian heretics must remain a matter of speculation apart from the concrete instance of *Reading I* in Adamantius, and this now has been challenged in turn by Aland. Not only does Aland date Adamantius' dialogue later than do Mehlmann and others, namely, about 325 or later, he demonstrates that, as with Alexander, the manuscripts containing the quoted material (and *Reading I*) from Adamantius are unreliable. The parallel Latin version of the relevant passage gives not *Reading I* but *Reading II*, and the manuscript basis of the Greek version itself of the dialogue is highly suspect, especially in the second part from which the scriptural quotation is taken.[17]

Aland himself is skeptical that *Reading I* could have arisen before the middle of the fourth century. He concedes that some witnesses for *Reading I* date earlier, but he believes that the unreliability of almost all of these

---

[11] Mehlmann, "A Note on John 1:3," p. 341.

[12] St. Augustine, *In Ioannis Evangelium*, I, 16 (*PL*, 35, 1387).

[13] Irenaeus, *Adversus Haereses*, I, 8, 5 (*PG*, 7, 553); Clement of Alexandria, *Excerpta ex Scriptis Theodoti*, 6 (*PG*, 9, 657).

[14] According to Irenaeus, *Adversus Haereses*, I, 8, 5f. (*PG*, 7, 533f.).

[15] Heracleon, *In Ioannis Evangelium*, II, 21.

[16] Cf. Haenchen, "Probleme des johanneischen 'Prologs,'" pp. 316ff.; also, Pagels, *The Johannine Gospel in Gnostic Exegesis*, esp. Chs. 1 and 2, and Wiles, *The Spiritual Gospel*, pp. 96ff.

[17] Aland, "Eine Untersuchung zu Joh. 1:3-4," pp. 197f.

testimonies can be either proved or rendered probable. *Reading I* was thought to appear, for example, in Cyprian's *Ad Quirinum*, II, 3 (*nondum vidi*). Aland's speculation that this punctuation must be the work of Cyprian's editor in 1868 (G. Hartel) is now supported by the 1972 edition (ed. R. Weber) which prints *Reading II*. In any case, as Aland observes, it would be difficult to reconcile a *Reading I* in Cyprian with no less than five instances of *Reading II* in the nearly contemporary Victorinus of Pettau, Lactantius, and Marius Victorinus. *Reading I* is claimed to occur three times in Eusebius. But Aland shows that the first of these (*De Laudibus Constantini*, 12, 7 (*PG*, 20, 1398)) involves an eleventh century correction, and that in the two others (*Praeparatio Evangelica*, VII, 12, 9 (*PG*, 21, 1543), and XI, 19, 3 (*PG*, 21, 900)) the editor's punctuation after ὃ γέγονεν (= *Reading I*) is doubtful since the second of these clearly requires *Reading II* when considered with its introductory context (XI, 19 1f. (*PG*, 21, 900)). In addition, it is to be noted that John 1:3 occurs in Eusebius no less than seventeen times and always with the impression of completeness: The whole of John 1:1-3 is quoted once and according to *Reading II*, on several occasions John 1:1 and 1:3 are quoted successively, ending always with οὐδὲ ἕν (= *Reading II*), and he quotes John 1:3 and 1:4 twice in one context, both times breaking off with οὐδὲ ἕν, inserting a brief comment, and resuming the quotation with ὃ γέγονεν (= *Reading II*). Aland regards this last as conclusive proof that *Reading II* is the reading employed by Eusebius. Didymus is sometimes cited as employing *Reading I* in the quotation of John 1:1-3 at *De Trinitate*, I, 15, 17 (*PG*, 39, 297), which is a lemma for the subsequent exposition at I, 15, 19 (*PG*, 39, 300). Now, whereas a copyist often enough transcribed a New Testament passage according to the text known by him, he might not so freely alter the text as it occurs in an author's exposition. Be that as it may, the text of John 1:3 in the lemma is given according to *Reading I*, but in Didymus' exposition it is given according to *Reading II*. In any event, if, as is disputed, Didymus is the author of this work, we find ourselves now already in the middle of the fourth century and in the midst of the Arian controversy.[18]

We are, then, with Aland, driven to the view that *Reading I* was originally motivated, after all, by a concern for the Arian employment of *Reading II*. It is evident from the quotation from Ambrose at the beginning of this section that *Reading I* had by his time been adapted by some unidentifiable "Alexandrians and Egyptians" as an anti-Arian measure. It seems impossible to pin-point *Reading I* any earlier or any more specifically. If so, then the first identifiable instance of *Reading I* is to be

---

[18] Aland, "Eine Untersuchung zu Joh. 1:3-4," pp. 198ff.

found in Epiphanius in the latter half of the fourth century.[19] Here, in *Adversus Octoginta Haereses*, LXIX, 56 (*PG*, 42, 289), *Reading I* and *Reading II* appear side by side, with Epiphanius appealing, at least, to the upstart *Reading I* as a way of combating the Pneumatomachi who were citing the short form of John 1:3 (i.e. *Reading II*) as evidence for their belief in the createdness of the Holy Spirit.

Given the welter of even pre-Arian misconstructions of *Reading II*, and, at best, the ambiguity of claimed extant instances of *Reading I* prior to Epiphanius, it would be quite impossible ever to identify with any assurance a pre-Arian context and motivation for the rise of *Reading I*. On the other hand, in view of the relevant extant sources and the analysis thereof (essentially Aland's analysis), we accept that in all probability *Reading I* began to emerge tentatively and at unknown hands as a polemic against the Arians' abuse of *Reading II*; it was then employed in a similar way by Epiphanius against the Pneumatomachi; soon after, Chrysostom too was tempted by it as a means of confounding false teaching, and Theodore Mopsuestia is found insisting on it as the correct reading; and it eventually hardened into the standard text, its original anti-Arian intent forgotten.

The purpose of the above historical-exegetical-theological excursus has been to show how *Reading II* of John 1:3/4 was recognized already in antiquity as the *lectio difficilior*. Inasmuch as ὃ γέγονεν was taken as referring to something created, *Reading II* played into the hands of a multitude of heretical Gnostic-type interpretations; inasmuch as ὃ γέγονεν ἐν αὐτῷ ζωὴ ἦν seemed to attribute or to relate createdness to the Logos, *Reading II* played into the hands of the Arian heresy, and it was probably as a corrective to this that *Reading I* arose, the *lectio proclivior*.

But the ancients have not been the only ones to reject *Reading II* because of the difficulties it poses. It is easy to show that many modern commentators likewise reject *Reading II* on the grounds that to take ὃ γέγονεν as referring to natural creation, or to anything created at all, is un-Johannine or indeed yields no sound theological sense whatsoever. Lagrange: *Reading II-B*, the early reading preferred by Gnostics, "est impossible, parce que Jo. n'a sûrement pas l'intention d'installer les créatures dans le Verbe."[20] Adolf Schlatter: *Reading I* makes more sense inasmuch as "die ζωή ist Besitz des Worts, nicht des Menschen oder der Natur."[21] Metzger: ". . . 'That which has been made in him was life'—whatever that may be supposed to mean."[22] Morris: *Reading II* "is not

[19] Thus Aland, "Eine Untersuchung zu Joh. 1:3-4," p. 200.
[20] M.-J. Lagrange, *Évangile selon Saint Jean*, third ed. (Paris: Gabalda, 1927), p. 6.
[21] A. Schlatter, *Der Evangelist Johannes*, p. 6.
[22] Metzger, *A Textual Commentary on the Greek New Testament*, p. 196.

easy to accept. That the Word is the source of life is a typically Johannine idea. That everything that has been made is life is not, even if we add 'in him.'"²³ Barrett: ". . . it makes much better, and more Johannine, sense to say that in the Word was life, than to say [on *Reading II*] that the created universe was life in him. . . ."²⁴ If we, like Barrett and these others, understand ὃ γέγονεν as an extension or restatement of the πάντα of vs. 3, then the statement is indeed theologically difficult, and it is precisely this difficulty (sometimes augmented by still others) that has led the scholars just mentioned, and many others, to opt rather for *Reading I*.

On the other hand, the rejection of *Reading II*, whether by ancients or moderns, because of the difficulties it poses is only so much more evidence, on the *lectio difficilior* principle, for its originality; it simply reinforces the linguistic and textual evidence presented earlier in support of *Reading II*. But with the heightened probability of *Reading II* as original the problem persists: Discounting the ancient heretical interpretations, is it possible to assign to John 1:4a, on *Reading II*, a plausible interpretation? Most commentators who accept *Reading II* have fabricated interpretations that are forced or farfetched, failing, by and large, to note a possible interpretation which not only explains most effectively the meaning of John 1:4a, but which also immediately illuminates both the theological perspective and hymnic character of John 1:1-5 and therefore the Prologue as a whole. But before we develop what we think is the most plausible interpretation of John 1:4a, on *Reading II*, it would be useful to consider some of the attempted, and, it turns out, *im*plausible interpretations.

Reading II: *Four Implausible Interpretations*

The attempts to make good theological and Johannine sense of *Reading II*—misguided, we think—may be collapsed generally into four. We will label these the (i) metaphysical, (ii) existential, (iii) naturalistic, and (iv) *imago Dei* interpretations. They overlap at certain points and they all have in common the opinion that ὃ γέγονεν in John 1:4a refers in some way to something created, if not to archetypal and transcendent creatures then to creatures of nature.

(i) Bultmann addresses briefly (and rejects) what is probably the most extreme of the "metaphysical" interpretations of John 1:4a (*Reading II*). This interpretation takes ἐν αὐτῷ with ὃ γέγονεν (*Reading II-A*, "What has come into being in him, was life") and construes vs. 4a as asserting "die

---

²³ Morris, *The Gospel according to John*, p. 82.
²⁴ Barrett, *The Gospel according to St. John*, p. 157.

ideale (Prä-)Existenz alles Geschaffenen im Logos."[25] This "spekulative Gedanke," as Bultmann notes, calls to mind Philo who represented the Logos as the κόσμος νωητός,[26] Plotinus who taught that the archetypal Ideas were located in νοῦς,[27] and the Hermetic writings where κόσμος is represented as a hypostatization of the πλήρωμα.[28] Against such a view Bultmann argues that it would require taking the ἐν of ἐν αὐτῷ instrumentally in light of the instrumental δι᾽ αὐτοῦ of vs. 3, and in that case it is enigmatic why δι᾽ αὐτοῦ was not employed also in vs. 4. That is, as Bultmann apparently intends, if we understand ὃ γέγονεν of vs. 4 to be parallel in meaning with πάντα of vs. 3, then we should expect the prepositions which follow to be parallel also, but they are not: πάντα (creation) through him (δι᾽ αὐτοῦ) . . . ὃ γέγονεν (creation) through him (ἐν αὐτῷ). Bultmann is right in his rejection of this interpretation but his reasoning falls short. First, it is no more required that the prepositions be parallel than that the expressions designating the creation are parallel; that is, if—which we do not in fact accept—the author could switch from πάντα to ὃ γέγονεν but retain the same meaning, he could also and as easily switch from διά to (an instrumental) ἐν while retaining the same meaning. Second, it is not required on the ideal-(pre-)existence theory that πάντα and ὃ γέγονεν do designate the same thing and thus there is no expectation that ἐν should parallel διά. Is it not at least possible (however doubtful) that the different prepositions suggest precisely the Philonic distinction between the world of ordinary things (πάντα) created through the Logos (vs. 3), and the archetypal Ideas (ὃ γέγονεν) created *in* and inhering *in* the Logos, the Divine Reason? Such an idea would be suggested by the following, and somewhat typical, statement from Philo: Ὁ μὲν οὖν ἀσώματος κόσμος ἤδη πέρας εἶχεν ἱδρυθεὶς ἐν τῷ θείῳ λόγῳ, ὁ δ᾽ αἰσθητὸς πρὸς παράδειγμα τούτου ἐτελειογονεῖτο.[29]

We too reject the interpretation before us (this "spekulative Gedanke") but, as will be seen, for different and additional reasons than the one given by Bultmann. Furthermore, this interpretation was projected by Bultmann as a possible or hypothetical one; as an actual interpretation of our passage it was never, as far as we can tell, proposed by anyone. That Philo, for example, *might* have interpreted the verse in this way *had* he been a Christian and *had* he commented on the passage verges on the irrelevant, to say the least. We will do better to attend to metaphysical interpretations which have actually been proposed and have been conse-

[25] Bultmann, *Das Evangelium des Johannes*, p. 21, n. 4.
[26] Philo, *De Opificio Mundi*, 24.
[27] Plotinus, *Enneads*, VI, 7, 8.
[28] *Hermetica*, XII, 15.
[29] Philo, *De Opificio Mundi*, 36.

quential in the history of the interpretation of the passage. Of these, there can be little doubt that it has been the Augustinian-type view that has dominated.

Let us consider, then, St. Augustine's own interpretation of the passage. Augustine's text of the first five verses of John read as follows:

(1) In principio erat verbum, et verbum erat apud Deum, et Deus erat verbum. (2) Hoc erat in principio apud Deum. (3) Omnia per ipsum facta sunt, et sine ipso factum est nihil. (4) Quod factum est, in ipso vita erat, et vita erat lux hominum. (5) Et lux in tenebris lucet, et tenebrae non comprehenderunt.

We are alerted to the speculative-metaphysical character of Augustine's exegesis long before we ever reach vs. 4. We learn for example that the opening words of his text, "in principio," denote at once the location or position of the Word "in" the Father, who is here called "principium," though the Father or the Word or both together may be regarded as "principium" relative to creatures;[30] that in any case time itself is a creature and therefore "principium" denotes not the temporal but the ontological beginning, that is, the ultimate origin or cause of all things;[31] that the last two propositions of vs. 1 demonstrate the distinction of persons ("verbum erat apud Deum") and identity of substance ("et Deus erat verbum") in the Trinity;[32] that the imperfect tense "erat" of vss. 1-2 and the perfect "facta sunt"/"factum est" of vss. 3-4 express the distinction between uncreated and created substance;[33] and, more generally, that the "verbum" is the perfect self-expression of Being Itself, the perfect *ratio* that subsists in God and is manifested imperfectly in the expression or image that is the world. Armed especially with the Platonic distinctions between Being and Becoming involved in this last point, Augustine is prepared for the exegesis of vs. 4.

Augustine acknowledges, as most have, the possibility of placing a comma either after "quod factum est" (*Reading II-B*) or after "in ipso" (*Reading II-A*), that is, the possibility of taking "in ipso" with what precedes or with what follows. He suggests, in fact, that we make a short pause after "quod factum est," and that we take the words "in ipso vita erat" together so as to avoid the Manichaean suggestion that all creation is possessed of divine life. That is, "quod factum est in ipso, vita erat" (*Reading II-A*) could suggest that creation itself possessed the divine life, whereas "quod factum est, in ipso vita erat" (*Reading II-B*) suggests a

---

[30] St. Augustine, *De Trinitate*, VI, 2 (*PL*, 42, 924f.); V, 13 (920).
[31] St. Augustine, *De Civitate Dei*, XI, 5 (*PL*, 41, 321).
[32] St. Augustine, *De Trinitate*, I, 6 (*PL*, 42, 825); VI, 2 (925).
[33] St. Augustine, *In Ioannis Evangelium*, I, 11f. (*PL*, 35, 1384f.).

distinction between creation and the divine life since creation was life by virtue of a relation or participation in the Word. But what, more exactly, is meant by "life"? Augustine understands "life" to mean here the archetypal "number, weight, and measure" (Wis. 11:21) or ideal, intelligible structure, imprinted on all creation from its divine origin. Thus, "that which was made, in him was life," expresses the fact that all creation participates in the divine *rationes*:

> Facta est terra, sed ipsa terra quae facta est, non est vita: est autem in ipsa Sapientia spiritualiter ratio quaedem qua terra facta est; haec vita est.[34]

The exemplarism involved in Augustine's interpretation shows even more clearly when he likens the world created by the Logos to a box fashioned by a carpenter and then distinguishes the box as it is in design ("in arte") and the box as it is in fact ("in opere"). He concludes,

> . . . quia Sapientia Dei, per quam facta sunt omnia, secundum artem continet omnia, antequam fabricet omnia; hinc quae fiunt per ipsam artem, non continuo vita sunt, sed quidquid factum est, vita in illo est. Terram vides; est in arte terra. Coelum vides; est in arte coelum. Solem et lunam vides; sunt et ista in arte. Sed foris corpora sunt, in arte vita sunt.[35]

For those who know Augustine there is nothing new or surprising in this view of creation. What is important at the moment is that these words were written as a commentary on John 1:4a.

Such an interpretation is not peculiar to St. Augustine. It dominated medieval exegeses of the passage and shows up, for example, also in St. Thomas. St. Thomas distinguished the being which created things have in themselves and the being which they have in the Word: In themselves they neither are nor have life, though considered as being made through the Word they are life in virtue of their relation to their divine archetypes existing in the Wisdom of God.[36]

Nor is this interpretation peculiar to antiquity. The modern scholar Westcott, for example, also proffers a very metaphysical and very Platonic view of the passage. It lifts us, he says, beyond the temporality of created things to their pre-existent and abiding ideas or essences in the Divine Mind. In this way, "that which was created and still continues" (ὃ γέγονεν), endures precisely because of its trans-temporal or essential rela-

---

[34] St. Augustine, *In Ioannis Evangelium*, I, 16 (*PL*, 35, 1387). Naturally, Augustine was fond of construing the Johannine Logos as the creative Wisdom of the Old Testament (cf. for example, Ps. 104:24; Prov. 3:19; 8:27ff.; Wis. 7:12; 8:4, 6, 27ff.; 9.9, Sir 24.5).

[35] St. Augustine, *In Ioannis Evangelium*, I, 17 (*PL*, 35, 1387).

[36] St. Thomas Aquinas, *Lectura super Johannem*, I, 2 (91).

tion (ἦν) to the divine life.[37] Westcott's platonizing is unmistakable when he says,

> . . . the thought of the reader is carried away from the present, and raised (so to speak) to the contemplation of the essence of things. For a moment we are taken from phenomena—"that which hath become"—to being, to the divine "idea" of things. . . .
> That which was created and still continues, represents to us what was beyond time (if we dare so speak) in the Divine Mind.[38]

and when he distinguishes ἐν αὐτῷ ζωὴ ἦν as the "idea" and ὃ γέγονεν as "the temporal realization of the idea," a contrast which he thinks appears a second time in the Johannine literature, specifically in the imperfect and aorist of the last line of the Hymn of the Elders in Rev. 4:11:

> Worthy art thou, our Lord and God,
> to receive glory and honor and power,
> for thou didst create all things,
> and by thy will they existed [ἦσαν] and were created [ἐκτίσθησαν].[39]

As we turn to the criticism of the metaphysical interpretation we may recall that this approach, as well as the following three, for its own reasons takes ὃ γέγονεν as referring to something created. Later we will be arguing for a radically different view of ὃ γέγονεν, and one which, if correct, renders the metaphysical interpretation of John 1:4a, and the following three interpretations too, impossible from the start.

For the moment, though, we may consider the following two lines of criticism. Because of the way in which the Augustinian-type interpretation identifies ὃ γέγονεν with the temporal world in contrast to the intelligible world designated by ἐν αὐτῷ ζωὴ ἦν, the metaphysical interpretation is required to opt for *Reading II-B*,[40] with the problematic punctuation, ὃ γέγονεν, ἐν αὐτῷ ζωὴ ἦν. *Reading II-B* though not impossibly clumsy is not quite grammatical either. It is true, as we noted in an earlier context, that the *casus pendens* construction is not uncommon in John. Nonetheless, one might find this interpretation unconvincing on the grounds alone that it involves the admittedly strained punctuation of *Reading II-B*. But this is not a decisive point.

Our second line of criticism is more important, though it is more general and subjective. It depends, admittedly, on a certain view as to the

---

[37] Westcott, *The Gospel according to St. John*, p. 30.
[38] Westcott, *The Gospel according to St. John*, p. 30.
[39] Westcott, *The Gospel according to St. John*, p. 30.
[40] We are thus excluding here the hypothetical interpretation noted by Bultmann and which involved *Reading II-A* discussed above.

general character of the Fourth Gospel—what it is about and not about, what intellectual and cultural categories conditioned the Evangelist's thought and what did not, what his purpose was and what it was not, and so on.

It is not for nothing that the Fourth Gospel and especially the Prologue is often called the most "philosophical" writing in the Bible. This usually refers in a general way to a certain loftiness of ideas and eloquence of expression, though it may extend also to specific ideas and concepts, as in the second and third propositions of the Prologue ("The Logos was with God, and the Logos was God") where we encounter a primitive expression of the divine ontology: the distinction of persons and the unity of substance.[41] In this respect Brown no doubt overstates the case when, in commenting on the first verses of John, he says,

> . . . there is not the slightest indication of interest in metaphysical speculations about relationships within God or in what later theology would call Trinitarian processions.[42]

Still, there are those who have wrung from the Prologue more philosophy than is actually there, and such "metaphysical" exegeses of vs. 4a as we have just mentioned are examples. Surely it strains the exegetical and historical sense to imagine that the "life" of vs. 4, as one scholar expresses it,

> refers to the way in which quantitative and qualitative multiplicity, including the multiplicity of temporal succession, coexists, and in God pre-exists eternally, in the unity of a Mind.[43]

In such talk, as well as talk about "transcendent essences" or "the participated life of the Word," one senses the imposition of speculative and metaphysical interests surely alien both to the Evangelist's thought and to his purpose.[44] We have already granted that such a judgment is to some degree subjective and impressionistic. But all of us operate sooner or later (and rightfully so) with the criterion of coherence, that is, the question

---

[41] We have seen above that such an interpretation is at least as old as Augustine. For a recent discussion and defense of this interpretation, see Ed. L. Miller, "The *Logos* was God," *EQ,* 53 (1981), esp. pp. 76f.

[42] Brown, *The Gospel according to St. John,* I, p. 23.

[43] William Carroll, "Saint Augustine on John 1:1-5" (unpublished), p. 8.

[44] On the specifically Augustinian view, Calvin is certainly correct: "Augustinus more suo nimium platonicus ad ideas rapitur: quod Deus antequam mundum conderet, formam totius opificii in mente sua conceptam habuerit: atque ita vita eorum quae nondum exstabant, in Christo fuerit, quia in eo ordinata erat mundi creatio. Sed quam istud sit a mente evangelistae longe remotum, mox videbimus." (John Calvin, *In Ioannis Evangelium,* I, 3).

as to what supports and is supported by, or what "fits," the sum total of our understanding.

(ii) We move, then, to the second type of interpretation of John 1:4a (*Reading II*), the "existential." Not surprisingly, Bultmann is the chief representative of this approach.[45] Bultmann also takes ἐν αὐτῷ with ζωὴ ἦν, that is, *Reading II-B.* He then declares that vs. 4a can mean, "What has come to be—in him (the Logos) was the life (for it)" or "What has come to be—in it he (the Logos) was the life." In either case, the real point, according to Bultmann, is that creation does not contain within itself the principle of life but possesses life by virtue of the "Lebenskraft" of the creating Logos. Vs. 4b then affirms the possibility of revelation given such a creation: This "life" of the Logos was the "light of men"— Bultmann takes τὸ φῶς τῶν ἀνθρώπων as an objective genitive, "the light for men (für die Menschen)."[46]

Especially from Bultmann's conception of light as revelation in vs. 4b it is not a big step to his existential interpretation of the entire verse. The existential slant is unmistakable in the following:

> . . . wenn er dies war als der Schöpfer, als die ζωή, so heisst das, dass in dem *Ursprung* der Existenz die Möglichkeit der *Erleuchtung* der Existenz, das Heil des definitiven Verständnisses ihrer selbst, gegeben war. Die Schöpfung ist zugleich Offenbarung, sofern das Geschaffene die Möglichkeit hatte, um seinen Schöpfer zu wissen und so sich selbst zu verstehen.[47]

> Im ursprünglichen Sinne ist Licht nicht ein Beleuchtungsapparat, der Dinge erkennbar macht, sondern die *Helligkeit*, in der ich mich je befinde und zurechtfinden kann, in der ich "aus und ein weiss" und keine Angst habe; die Heiligkeit also nicht als ein äusseres Phänomen, sondern als Erhelltsein des Daseins, meiner selbst.[48]

> . . . wie zum "Leben" das definitive Sich-Verstehen gehört, das keine Frage, kein Rätsel mehr kennt, so gehört zu dem "Licht," das der Mensch als dieses definitive Erleuchtetsein ersehnt, die Freiheit vom Tode als dem Schicksal, das das Dasein schlechthin unverständlich macht.[49]

> Der Zusammenhang von Licht und Leben ist ja sachlich damit gegeben, dass Leben seine Eigentlichkeit gewinnt im echten Verständnis seiner selbst.[50]

---

[45] In contrast to the stance taken in his commentary, Bultmann had earlier regarded ὃ γέγονεν as a gloss affixed to the end of vs. 3 (cf. "Der religionsgeschichtliche Hintergrund des Prologs zum Johannesevangelium," in *EΥΧΑΡΙΣΤΗΡΙΟΝ: Studien zur Religion und Literatur des Alten und Neuen Testaments*, ed. Hans Schmidt (Göttingen: Vandenhoeck & Ruprecht, 1923), II, p. 4, n. 2).

[46] Bultmann, *Das Evangelium des Johannes*, pp. 20ff.

[47] Bultmann, *Das Evangelium des Johannes*, p. 25.

[48] Bultmann, *Das Evangelium des Johannes*, p. 22.

[49] Bultmann, *Das Evangelium des Johannes*, p. 24.

[50] Bultmann, *Das Evangelium des Johannes*, p. 26.

Thus for Bultmann John 1:4 expresses the existentially revelatory character of creation: It provides *Erhelltsein des Daseins* and the consequent *existen-
tielles Selbstverständnis*.

Like the metaphysical interpretation, this existential interpretation
connects John 1:4a with the preceding vs. 3, that is, it refers ὃ γέγονεν to
things created. Again, this is a crucial assumption—mistake, we think—
and will be considered later. Also, it is not necessary to rehearse again the
objections to the strained punctuation involved in *Reading II-B*, which in
turn is required by the existential interpretation of Bultmann, though it
should be noted how either of Bultmann's two renderings of *Reading II-B*
involve parenthetical, explanatory expressions, which have not the
slightest bases in the text. In addition, Bultmann's interpretation requires
that the existentially revelatory "light" exists and is operative prior to the
incarnation of the Logos. This is apparent from the first quotation above,
and elsewhere he states it explicitly: "Das Licht scheint in die Finsternis,
auch ehe das Fleisch ward (1:5)."[51] But such a claim will have no small
difficulty squaring itself with John's pervasive use of "light" throughout
his Gospel in consistent reference to the *incarnate* Logos. From a logical,
philological, and stylistic standpoint, it would be arbitrary not to take the
"light" of vs. 5 as synonymous with the "light" of vs. 4, and in vs. 4
"light" is equated with "life." We will argue in the ensuing discussion of
the "naturalistic" interpretation of vs. 4a (*Reading II*) that these terms
surely must mean here what they mean elsewhere throughout John's
Gospel, namely, the spiritual and salvific life and light that are encountered
in the incarnate Logos. But particularly relevant at this point in our
discussion are 3:19, 12:35-36, 46, and especially 9:5: "When I am in the
world, I am the light of the world." Bultmann's claim that the light in vss.
4-5 is a pre-incarnate light must be rejected. Closely related to this is
Demke's charge that Bultmann's equation of creation with revelation
("die Schöpfung ist zugleich Offenbarung") is a too hasty identification:
It arrests the slant of these verses which, true to Johannine usage, narrows
the whole of creation (vs. 3) to what κόσμος primarily means to John,
namely, mankind (vs. 4b).[52]

Finally, as in the case of the metaphysical interpretation, our main
criticism of the existential interpretation is more general. It is to be
rejected because it, like the metaphysical interpretation, commits us to a
philosophical perspective (this time to an existential one) which was
surely alien to the Evangelist's mind and purpose. In a useful article on

---

[51] Rudolf Bultmann, "Die Eschatologie des Johannes-Evangeliums," *Glauben und Verstehen: Gesammelte Aufsätze*, I (Tübingen: Mohr, 1933), p. 138.

[52] Demke, "Der sogenannte Logos-Hymnus im johanneischen Prolog," pp. 55f. See also the problems which Demke sees generated for vs. 5 by Bultmann's stance (pp. 56f.).

Bultmann's interpretation of John 1:3-4, Kysar summarizes the existential pre-understanding involved in Bultmann's interpretation of these verses as (1) the anthropocentric understanding of all Christian doctrine, (2) the theme of human dependence, (3) the unity of the concepts of creation and redemption in Christian thought, and (4) the character of natural revelation as self-understanding.[53] Kysar is no doubt right that (as in the case of Bultmann, though it applies as easily to St. Augustine and anyone else) "it is impossible for [the exegete] to understand a text without contributing to that understanding his own theological presuppositions," and it is true that

> only an exegetical method aware of itself, its own presuppositions and internal logic is capable of anything approaching faithful interpretation of the text.[54]

But it is also clear (what Kysar does not quite say) that having distinguished and understood one's own "world of meaning" in relation to that of the text, one must not allow the latter to be distorted by the former. The hermeneutical endeavor must never in principle allow for the confusion of "the worlds of meaning," however difficult it may be in practice to keep them distinct.

In this respect Bultmann has often and rightly been criticized. It is not a matter of his existential reinterpretation of the Biblical documents, but rather a matter of the imposition of his own ideas onto the writers of the New Testament to the point of distorting and misrepresenting theirs. The present instance is a noteworthy example. Here it is not a matter of reinterpreting in existential terms a sort of demythologized version of John 1:3-4, but of attributing to the Evangelist himself at this point the existentialist perspective. It is doubtful that John had read Plato, but it is certain that he never read Heidegger! Just as we did not earlier deny utterly the metaphysical import of the verses before us, neither do we now deny their existential import. They do indeed have to do ultimately with the call to decision, or, more specifically, with the one about whom we must decide. But beyond this we must be on guard not to force upon these words an unnatural and alien meaning. For our part, it is as difficult to see in these words a doctrine of existential *Selbstverständnis* as a doctrine of Platonic Ideas or the like.

(iii) We come to the third type of interpretation of John 1:4a (*Reading II*), the "naturalistic." As one may guess, according to this view the ζωή,

---

[53] R. Kysar, "R. Bultmann's Interpretation of the Concept of Creation in John 1:3-4: A study of exegetical method," *CBQ* 32 (1970), p. 80.

[54] Kysar, "R. Bultmann's Interpretation of the Concept of Creation in John 1:3-4," p. 85.

and also the φῶς, of John 1:4 are understood either in their usual and most literal sense (the biological life of living things and the light emanating from the sun, moon, and stars), or, at least in the case of φῶς, in some metaphorical sense but still referring to natural capacities or faculties possessed by created things (reason, moral consciousness, etc.). That ζωή and/or φῶς refer here to natural endowments of creatures has been, no doubt, the most widely accepted interpretation both on *Reading I* and on *Reading II*. It was adopted generally by the Fathers[55] and by the majority of commentators ever since.[56] These almost always see Ps. 36:9 as relevant background for the interpretation of the passage:

> For with thee is the fountain of life;
> in thy light do we see light.

Here, of course, we are only interested in this naturalistic interpretation as it bears on John 1:4a according to *Reading II*. MacGregor provides an explicit example, reflecting specifically *Reading II-B*:

> . . . through the activity of the Logos the life-principle first appeared in the world. . . . this seems a perfectly acceptable interpretation: . . . "as for creation, in it the Logos was the principle of life . . . and this life . . . was the light of men." . . . from the Creative Logos springs life in its most perfect

---

[55] For a survey, see Julianus Gennaro, *Exegetica in Prologum Joannis sec. Maximos Ecclesiae Doctores Antiquitatis Christianae* (Rome: Pontificium Athenaeum Antonianum, 1952), Ch. 2, and I. de la Potterie, "De Punctuatie en de Exegese van Joh. 1:3-4 in de Traditie," *Bijdragen*, 16 (1955), pp. 117ff.

[56] A good example is John Calvin who takes ζωή in vs. 4a to be the *continua inspiratio* of the world: ". . . simplex enim sensus est, sermonem Dei non modo fontem vitae fuisse creaturis omnibus, ut esse inciperent quae nondum erant: sed vivifica eius virtute fieri ut in statu suo maneant. Nisi enim continua eius inspiratio mundum vegetet, necesse erit quaecunque vigent, protinus decidere, aut in nihilum redigi. Denique quod Paulus, Act. 17 v. 28, Deo adscribit, nos scilicet in ipso esse et moveri et vivere, Ioannnes sermonis beneficio fieri testatur. Deus ergo est qui nos vivificat: sed per aeternum sermonem." He takes the φῶς of vs. 4b to augment the thought so as to include natural reason: "Hic meo iudicio partem vitae commemorat, qua homines reliquis animantibus praecellunt: ac si diceret non vulgarem hominibus datam fuisse vitam, sed quae cum luce intelligentiae coniuncta esset." (*In Ioannis Evangelium*, I, 4)). More recent examples of the naturalistic interpretation in varying forms: Albin August Van Hoonacker, "Le Prologue du Quatrième Évangile," *RHE*, 2 (1901), pp. 5ff.; Bernard, *The Gospel according to St. John*, I, pp. 4f.; G. H. C. MacGregor, *The Gospel of John* (Garden City, N. Y.: Doubleday, 1929), pp. 6f.; Schlier, "Im Anfang war das Wort," p. 278; John Marsh, *The Gospel of St. John* (Baltimore, Md.: Penguin Books, 1968), p. 104; Boismard, *Le Prologue de Saint Jean*, pp. 29ff.; Lindars, *The Gospel of John*, pp. 85f.; Schnackenburg, *Das Johannesevangelium*, I, p. 217ff.; Morris, *The Gospel according to John*, pp. 82ff.; and Theobald, *Im Anfang war das Wort*, pp. 19f., 105, 120f. Many commentators fail to distinguish clearly between natural and supernatural life and light, or between two different grades of supernatural life and light, and produce, therefore, an obscure and confused interpretation (see below, n. 69).

development for every form of existence according to its measure (cf. Acts 17:28, "in him we live and move and exist").

. . . That life, which for all things else was but the fountain of existence, for man, as a rational and moral being, contained the promise of *light.* . . . In the case of man the ideal life manifests itself specially in the *knowledge of moral good*, a gift accessible only to the possessor of both reason and conscience, the two faculties which distinguish man from the rest of creation.[57]

Among those maintaining the naturalistic interpretation of *Reading II*, Van Hoonacker, Boismard, and de la Potterie provide perhaps the starkest and most sustained defense of it. Like those mentioned already, all three take ἐν αὐτῷ with what follows—*Reading II-B*. Van Hoonacker understood the antecedent of ἐν αὐτῷ not to be the Logos but rather ὃ γέγονεν: "What has begun to be, in that there was life." "Life" is here understood by Van Hoonacker as that natural life possessed by all creation from the start. Likewise, in the next line, "and the life was the light of men," "light" is understood naturalistically as illuminating the world and providing life and sustenance for men. It is not John the Baptist but rather this natural light, says Van Hoonacker, which is contrasted with the true light or the Logos is vs. 9.[58]

Boismard strengthens this last point by marshalling the facts that elsewhere in John the "true" bread is contrasted with natural bread (6:32) and that the "true" vine is a spiritual one (15:1). He offers some further evidence for Van Hoonacker's naturalistic interpretation of John 1:4: (1) It renders the first five verses of the Prologue exactly parallel to the creation account in Genesis; (2) it would be inappropriate to say of the "true" light that "the darkness has not overcome it" (vs. 5) inasmuch as spiritual darkness *must* disappear when the true light appears (I John 2:8)—it cannot coexist with the true light; and (3) it would be more consistent with John's expression elsewhere to speak rather of the "light of the world" than "the light of men" if the spiritual light of the Word is intended. Boismard thus believes that Van Hoonacker's interpretation of John 1:4 is possible, at least with the condition that the natural life and light there spoken of be taken as a figure and type of the true light, the Word.[59]

In fact, however, Boismard believes that ἐν αὐτῷ refers not to the created order ("in it") but to the Logos ("in him"). His own interpretation—nonetheless naturalistic—takes a somewhat different form:

---

[57] MacGregor, *The Gospel of John*, pp. 6f.
[58] Van Hoonacker, "Le Prologue du Quatrième Évangile," pp. 5ff.
[59] Boismard, *Le Prologue de Saint Jean*, pp. 29ff.

Tout ce qui est devenu en Lui est vie, c'est-à-dire: tout ce qui a été créé est vie dans le Verbe, vient puiser sa vie dans le Verbe; et si le Verbe est appelé Vie, c'est précisément parce qu'il est la source de la vie pour tout ce qui vit au sein de la création.[60]

This means, as Boismard himself observes, that in one breath John speaks of life as the participated or created life of creatures ("What has begun to be, in him was life") and then in the next breath of the uncreated life of the Logos ("and the life was the light of men"), inasmuch as life is identified with the light, and the light clearly refers to the Logos. But he believes that the immediate transition from the idea of infused life to the idea of uncreated life (or *vice versa*) is otherwise found in John, for example at I John 1:2/5:13 and at 5:11-12.[61]

In his 1955 study, de la Potterie rejects the metaphysical exemplarism involved in most medieval exegeses of the passage ("merito nunc . . . ab omnibus rejicitur"[62]) and, following the exegesis of Cyril of Alexandria, Ambrosiaster, and John Scotus Eriugena, furthers the naturalistic interpretation in a way very similar to Boismard: "What has been made, in the Word was life," because the life of creatures has its permanent cause in the Word which is immanent to them; thus creatures participate in the life of the Word itself. And he too argues that as we pass from vs. 4a of *Reading II-B*: Even though the anarthrous ζωή cannot be the subject of the creating Logos to the uncreated life of the Logos himself which the Logos confers upon men. He appeals to I John 1:2-3 and 5:11 as evidence for the bestowal of divine life and for the restriction of this to men, both of which ideas he believes illumines the meaning of John 1:4b.[63]

A still more recent variation may be mentioned. Gese has defended the naturalistic interpretation of vs. 4a by means specifically of the grammar of *Reading II-B:* Even though the anarthrous ζωή cannot be the subject of the clause, neither can ὃ γέγονεν since the life referred to is not merely biological but "das Lebens-Prinzip der Schöpfung" effected by the Logos; the subject must therefore be implicit in the ἦν and refer to the Logos (as in vss. 9 and 10), and must thus take up the *casus pendens*, ὃ γέγονεν (= *Reading II-B*). This yields what Gese calls the only possible understanding of vs. 4a: "What has been made, in it was he (the Logos) the life."[64]

[60] Boismard, *Le Prologue de Saint Jean*, p. 32.
[61] Boismard, *Le Prologue de Saint Jean*, p. 31f.
[62] De la Potterie, "De Interpunctione et Interpretatione Versuum Joh. 1:3-4," p. 206.
[63] De la Potterie, "De Interpunctione et Interpretatione Versuum Joh. 1:3-4," pp. 206ff.
[64] Gese, "Der Johannesprolog," p. 163.

Again, it will be noted that the naturalistic interpretation identifies ὃ γέγονεν in John 1:4a with the πάντα (= creation) in vs. 3. And again we postpone for the time being a critical discussion of this equation. For the moment, our first criticism of this general view is familiar by now. Like the earlier two interpretations, this one requires *Reading II-B* with the punctuation, ὃ γέγονεν, ἐν αὐτῷ ζωὴ ἦν. We have seen repeatedly that this is problematic. For Vawter it appears to be not only problematic but decisive evidence against the naturalistic interpretation:

> The difficulty that I see with this interpretation [*Reading II-B*] . . . is that it makes Jn say quite awkwardly a thing that we would expect him to put much more clearly. If he meant that whatever lives has had or has found its life in the Word, and that alone, why did he not say so? To extract this meaning it is necessary to supply connectives or to paraphrase radically. . . .[65]

In any event, we will see that *Reading II-B*, common to all of these interpretations of John 1:4a, is hardly forced upon us, and even if it were, the interpretation of ὃ γέγονεν as referring to creation, also common to all of these interpretations, certainly is not. We will argue later that a quite different and perfectly good sense may be accorded both to *Reading II-A* and *Reading II-B*.

The more serious objection to the naturalistic interpretation of John 1:4, *Reading II*, will require an extended discussion. This general interpretation must be credited in that it avoids the flamboyant philosophical appeals involved in the previous two. It sins, however, in the opposite direction of *under*estimating the terms and concepts involved here. The terms ζωή, "life," and φῶς, "light," occur pervasively in John's Gospel and First Epistle, and far more times than in any other New Testament writing.[66] More important, by means of these terms John represents ideas which are central to his theological and Christological perspective and purpose. We may even say that in the Johannine literature these are technical terms.[67]

---

[65] Vawter, "What Came to Be in Him Was Life (Jn. 1:3b- 4a)," p. 403.

[66] Ζωή forty-seven times, as opposed to the next highest number of thirteen in Romans; φῶς twenty-nine times, as opposed to eight in Acts.

[67] From the plenitude of literature, the following may be cited on the Johannine concepts of Life and/or Light: Brown, *The Gospel according to John*, I, pp. 505ff., 515f.; Schnackenburg, *Das Johannesevangelium*, II, Exc. 12; Rudolf Bultmann, "Ζωή (E.6)," in *TWNT*, II, pp. 871ff.; Hans Conzelmann, "Φῶς (E. IV.1)," in *TWNT*, IX, pp. 341ff.; C. H. Dodd, *The Interpretation of the Fourth Gospel* (Cambridge, England: Cambridge University Press, 1953), Part 2, Chs. 2, 7; Alf Correll, *Consummatum Est: Eskatologi och Kyrka i Johannesevangeliet* (Stockholm: Svenska Kyrkans Diakonistyrelses Bokförlag, 1950), pp. 139ff.; Floyd V. Filson, "The Gospel of Life: A Study in the Gospel of John," in *Current Issues in New Testament Interpretation*, ed. William Klassen and Graydon F. Snyder (New York: Harper & Row, 1962), pp. 111ff.; J. C. Coetzee, "Life (Eternal Life) in John's

We consider first ζωή, "life." It is not for nothing that the Gospel of John has often been called "the Gospel of Life." "Life" has been identified, with some justification, as "the most encompassing and significant word in this Gospel."[68] The fact is, though, that (setting aside the present instances in 1:4) ζωή in the Johannine Gospel and Epistles never designates natural, physical life; it always designates the spiritual, salvific, or "eternal" life[69] accessible in Jesus the Christ.[70]

Clearly this is so in John's statement of the very purpose of his writing,

> . . . these are written that you may believe that Jesus is the Christ, the Son of God, and that believing you may have life in his name (John 20:31).

and seemingly innumerable other instances, such as,

> . . . the words that I have spoken to you are spirit and life (John 6:63).

> . . . I came that they may have life, and have it abundantly (John 10:10).

> I am the way, and the truth, and the life (John 14:6).

If it is not self-evident from such "life-sayings" themselves, surely it is clear from their contexts that the life in view is not physical or natural life but spiritual or eternal life. To this it may be added that John uses ζωή, "life," and ζωὴ αἰώνιος, "eternal life," nearly an equal number of times (in the Gospel, eighteen and sixteen times respectively), and, more important, he uses them interchangeably,[71] as is evident from the

---

Writings and the Qumran Scrolls," *Neotestamentica*, 6 (1972), pp. 48ff.; D. George Vanderlip, *Christianity according to John* (Philadelphia: Westminster Press, 1975), Ch. 2; Franz Mussner, *ΖΩΗ: Die Anschauung vom "Leben" im vierten Evangelium unter Berücksichtigung der Johannesbriefe* (Munich: Fink, 1952); J. P. Weisengoff, "Light and Its Relation to Life in Saint John," *CBQ*, 8 (1946), pp. 48ff.

[68] Vanderlip, *Christianity according to John*, p. 31. But see especially Coetzee, "Life (Eternal Life) in John's Writings and the Qumran Scrolls," pp. 48ff.

[69] In order to clarify a possible terminological misunderstanding, let me stipulate that in the present contexts by "spiritual life" I mean the life imparted to the believer supernaturally through the Spirit (cf. John 3:5-7; 6:63) as opposed to the natural life possessed by humans, though this latter too may with some appropriateness be called "spiritual" or "divine" in order to distinguish it from that of lower creatures. Terminology aside, what is essential to the naturalistic interpretation is that life (and light) is ascribed to all creation, or at least to all human beings, whereas Johannine life (and light) is the possession only of those who believe in Jesus.

[70] For useful discussions of this point, see Vanderlip, *Christianity according to John*, pp. 32ff., and Coetzee, "Life (Eternal Life) in John's Writings and the Qumran Scrolls," pp. 50f. Note also Vawter's brief but forceful statement, "What Came to Be in Him Was Life (Jn. 1:3b-4a)," p. 404. A case may be made too for John's consistent use of the verb ζάω with the meaning "to live spiritually." This meaning may be insisted on even at John 4:46 and certainly 11:25-26 (cf. Corell, *Consummatum Est*, p. 139). At worst, these latter are exceptions which prove the rule.

[71] *Contra*, for example, Bultmann who distinguishes between ζωή and ζωὴ αἰώνιος (*Das Evangelium des Johannes*, p. 21, n. 3). Dodd claims, correctly, that the former is an abbreviation of the latter (*The Interpretation of the Fourth Gospel*, p. 144).

instances where they both occur within the same saying. A few examples:

> He who believes in the Son has eternal life; he who does not obey the Son shall not see life, but the wrath of God rests upon him (John 3:36).

> . . . he who hears my word and believes him who sent me, has eternal life; he does not come into judgment, but has passed from death to life (John 5:24).

> You search the scriptures, because you think that in them you have eternal life; and it is they that bear witness to me; yet you refuse to come to me that you may have life (John 5:39-40).

> . . . this is the testimony, that God gave us eternal life, and this life is in his Son (I John 5:11).

But the reverse side of this coin further seals the point. Not only does John *not* distinguish between ζωή and ζωὴ αἰώνιος, he *does* distinguish between ζωή, "life," and ψυχή, which he appears to use frequently to designate "natural" or "physical life," as in John 10:11, 15, 17; 13:37-38; 15:13; and I John 3:16. Especially striking is John 12:25, where ψυχή as natural life is contrasted with ζωή as eternal life in the same saying:

> He who loves his life (ψυχὴν) loses it, and he who hates his life (ψυχὴν) in this world will keep it for eternal life (ζωὴν αἰώνιον).

Further, it is significant that whereas John nowhere intimates that ζωή is the possession of everyone,[72] he does emphasize that it is the gift of God through faith, as in John 3:16 and 20:31.

From such considerations it would require not a little self-assurance to claim that ζωή in John 1:4 means not spiritual or eternal life but natural or physical life! But the case against the naturalistic interpretation of John 1:4 can be made even stronger. Relevant here is the further "life-saying,"

> . . . as the Father has life in himself, so he has granted the Son also to have life in himself (John 5:26).

The reference is, again, to spiritual and eternal life (as the context makes clear, if it is not clear already), and it is difficult to resist the suggestion that the reference here to life in the Son is theologically connected with

---

[72] John 1:9 is no exception. The phrase, "the true light which illuminates everyone," means either the exposing light of judgment (cf. 3:19-21) or the light which dispels spiritual darkness for those who choose to walk in it (cf. 8:12). In any event, Vawter argues that the point of the verse is not who or how many are illuminated by the light, but rather that this light which illuminates is the true one ("What Came to Be in Him Was Life (Jn. 1:3b-4a)," p. 405). Actually, the point of the verse is the *incarnation* of the true light: "The true light, which illuminates every man, was coming into the world." See below, p. 84 and n. 118.

the reference to life in the Logos in John 1:4a, "What has come about in him was life." It is almost impossible to believe that these two statements, at least at the point concerning life, do not involve the same fundamental idea, or, indeed, on the naturalistic interpretation of vs. 4a, that they involve two radically different concepts of "life." We may argue similarly for a loose parallelism between John 1:4a, "What has come about in him was life," and I John 1:2:

> . . . the life was made visible, and we have seen and witness and proclaim to you the eternal life which was with the Father and was made manifest to us. . . .

Now there is an obvious literary and theological connection between the Prologue of John and the first four verses of I John. The similarity in both the ideas and expressions is striking, and I John 1:1-4 (itself a sort of prologue to the Epistle) is certainly either an echo of the Prologue to the Gospel (if composed later) or in some ways a model for it (if, as I believe, it was composed earlier). The significant point here is that in I John 1:2 the "life," which appears to be in every way parallel to the "life" in John 1:4, is clearly designated as "the eternal life."

In sum: It would seem beyond dispute that ζωή can be conceived no differently here than elsewhere in the Gospel of John[73]—and, we might add, the First Epistle.

As for φῶς, "light" in John 1:4, clearly it must go the same way as "life" in view of the equation, "the life was the light of men."[74] Even if, *per impossible*, every other occurrence of "light" in John carried the meaning of natural, physical light, the "light" of John 1:4 would have to be interpreted in connection with the "life" with which it is there identified. In fact, however, φῶς elsewhere in John's Gospel and Epistles designates natural light in one passage only, John 11:9-10.[75] In all others of the many instances it designates the spiritual and salvific light which appears with the incarnate Logos. For example:

> . . . this is the judgment, that the light has come into the world, and men loved darkness rather than light, because their deeds were evil (John 3:19).

> When I am in the world, I am the light of the world (John 9:5).

---

[73] So also Aland, "Eine Untersuchung zu Joh. 1:3-4," p. 207.

[74] The absolute identification and interchangeability of the terms is guaranteed by the definite article with both ζωή and φῶς: Grammatically it is impossible to distinguish subject and predicate.

[75] Conzelmann's comment that one cannot always distinguish clearly between the figurative and the literal sense of "light" ("Φῶς (E. IV.1)," in *TWNT*, IX, p. 341) must seem to careful readers of John as simply false. Even the one passage he cites as an example of John's vacillation between the meanings of daylight and spiritual light (John 12:35) obviously refers to spiritual light.

The light is with you for a little longer. Walk while you have the light, lest darkness overtake you. . . . While you have the light, believe in the light, that you may become sons of light (John 12:35-36).

I have come as a light into the world, that whoever believes in me may not remain in darkness (John 12:46).

. . . God is light and in him is no darkness at all (I John 1:5).

Especially important is the following saying with its conjunction of "life" and "light":

I am the light of the world. He who follows me will not walk in darkness, but will have the light of life (John 8:12).

Many, including myself, take the last clause, τὸ φῶς τῆς ζωῆς, as involving a genitive of definition, "the light that is life," and the phrase as parallel in meaning to the identification in John 1:4b, "the life was the light of men."[76]

But is it really necessary to go beyond the immediate context of John 1:4 in order to exclude the naturalistic interpretation of "life" and "light" there? Van Hoonacker's interpretation took "life" and "light" in vs. 4 to refer to natural life and light, arguing that spiritual (life and) light is not introduced until vs. 7. Aside from the literary and logical problem posed by the suggestion that, in spite of the similar or identical language, vss. 4-5 refer to natural creation whereas vss. 7ff. refer to spiritual creation, it violates exegetical credulity to believe that the expression "the light of men" in vs. 4 thus means something so radically different from "the true light that illuminates every man" in vs. 9.[77] But even more immediately, surely "light" signifies a spiritual principle already in vs. 5: "The light shines in the darkness, and the darkness has not overcome it." If it is not obvious from the whole Fourth Gospel that what is in view here is the typically Johannine spiritual dualism of Light/Darkness (with its contrast and even struggle), one should attend to the (parallel?) idea expressed in

---

[76] In no case can we accept an interpretation like Schnackenburg's: "Der Ausdruck 'Licht des Lebens' bezeichnet zunächst das physische, irdische Leben, dessen sich der Mensch im Licht der Sonne erfreut . . . aber da dieses Leben von Gott geschenkt ist und im Angesicht Gottes gelebt wird, gewinnt es auch eine tiefere religiöse Bedeutung. . . ." (*Das Johannesevangelium*, I, p. 217f., n. 3). Aside from the question whether such a distinction would be interesting to John, Schnackenburg's comment surely places the emphasis in the wrong place. And even so, "religiöse Bedeutung" is too weak for John's idea which is not just religious but Christological and salvific.

[77] Loisy, in the first edition of his work, criticized Van Hoonacker in this very way, noting also that John echoes the language of Gen. 1, though not the ideas, and that it would be contrary to the character of Johannine symbolism to place an account of natural creation beside an account of spiritual creation (*Le Quatrième Évangile* (Paris: Picard, 1903), p. 160, n. 3).

I John 2:8: ". . . the darkness is passing away and the true light is already shining." it strains both literary and theological sense to think that in the reference immediately preceding, "light" means rather a natural, physical principle (the continuity of vss. 4 and 5, if it is not evident anyway, is suggested by the connective καί). And since in vs. 4b spiritual "light" is identified with "life," the latter too must be understood as a spiritual principle.

It may be recalled, though, that Boismard and de la Potterie, while they take the "life" in vs. 4b to be spiritual or divine life, take the "life" in vs. 4a to be natural or created life. Even Boismard felt the implausibility of this and posed the question which we ourselves would pose: "Saint Jean a-t-il pu employer le mot *vie* en deux sens différents, dans deux versets successifs?"[78] He answered "Yes," but the answer is surely "No." It is as impossible to pass immediately from natural life in vs. 4a to spiritual life in vs. 4b as it is to pass from spiritual light in vs. 4b to natural light in vs. 5. As for Boismard's appeal to I John 1:2/5:13 and 5:11-12 as involving ideas of both "uncreated" and "infused" life, those passages have to do only with the spiritual or eternal life that is the Logos and possessed by believers and have nothing to do with the natural life of all creatures as Boismard thinks is involved in John 1:4a. For that matter, Boismard's whole discussion is marred by his failure to distinguish clearly and rigorously between the natural life of all creatures and the spiritual or eternal life of believers, even if, as he thinks, such a distinction were found in John—which it is not. Thus, in de la Potterie's employment of I John 1:2-3 and 5:11 as controlling the interpretation of John 1:4b, his only mistake is not allowing those passages to control the interpretation of John 1:4a also.[79]

It might be noted in passing that in John 1:4b the equation or interchangeability implied by the articular nominatives on both sides of the copula, καὶ ἡ ζωὴ ἦν τὸ φῶς,[80] precludes such a notion as A. Schlatter's

---

[78] Boismard, *Le Prologue de Saint Jean*, p. 31.

[79] See also H. van den Bussche's response to de la Potterie: "Quod Factum Est, in Ipso Vita Erat (Jo. 1:3-4)," *Collationes Brugenses et Grandavenses*, 2 (1956), pp. 85ff. On both Boismard and de la Potterie, see Lacan, "L'Oeuvre du Verbe Incarné: Le Don de la Vie," *RSR*, 45 (1957)," pp. 65ff.

[80] This grammatical point is not sufficiently emphasized in F. Blass and A. Debrunner, *A Greek Grammar of the New Testament and Other Early Christian Literature*, tr. and rev. Robert W. Funk (Chicago: University of Chicago Press, 1961), sect. 273. But cf. Herbert Weir Smyth, *Greek Grammar*, rev. Gordon M. Messing (Cambridge, Mass.: Harvard University Press, 1959), sect. 1152; also A. T. Robertson, *A Grammar of the Greek New Testament in Light of Historical Research*, fourth ed. (New York: Hodder & Stoughton, 1923), pp. 767f. On the possibility of taking, indeed, φῶς rather than ζωὴ as the subject, see Boismard, *Le Prologue de Saint Jean*, pp. 32f.

that the successive expressions ὃ γέγονεν, ζωή, and φῶς yield an "aufsteigende Linie": existence, life, and awareness.[81] It also precludes Bauer's suggestion that life here is the "Mittel der Erleuchtung."[82] Grammar aside, this latter would seem clearly to dilute John's straightforward affirmation. Furthermore, such an interpretation must deal with the genitive of that other Johannine expression already considered, "the light of life" (John 8:12).

It is, of course, yet possible that in John 1:4 ζωή and φῶς were intended to suggest natural, physical life and light. But in view of John's use of these terms and ideas elsewhere and frequently throughout his Gospel and Epistles and the Prologue itself, there is created, I think, a considerable burden on those wishing to demonstrate a naturalistic meaning of these terms in John 1:4.[83] And the burden is not lifted any by those supporting observations of Boismard cited earlier. These either beg the question (as in Boismard's expectation that John 1:1-5 should exactly parallel the Genesis account of creation), or demand an overly scrupulous expression on the part of John (as in his claim that it would be meaningless for John to speak of spiritual darkness overcoming, or not, spiritual light, inasmuch as they cannot coexist), or insist on an overwrought consistency (as in his claim that "light of the world" rather that "light of men" would be a more Johannine expression for spiritual light). Not one of these nor

---

[81] A. Schlatter, *Der Evangelist Johannes*, p. 7.

[82] Bauer, *Das Johannesevangelium*, p. 11.

[83] Cf. Karl Barth's excellent summarizing comment from his Münster and Bonn lectures on John in 1925/1933 (*Erklärung des Johannes-Evangeliums (Kapitel 1-8)*, ed. Walther Fürst (Zürich: Theologischer Verlag, 1976), pp. 47f.):

. . . als mir im ganzen Johannes-Evangelium keine Stelle bekannt ist, wo es möglich wäre, für ζωή so etwas wie "anderes Sein hervorbringendes Sein," Leben aller Dinge in der Idee, continua inspiratio, allgemeiner Lebensquell usf. einzusetzen. Sondern durchweg in unserem Evangelium hat der Begriff ζωή (mit oder ohne Zusatz von αἰώνιος) soteriologisch-eschatalogische Bedeutung. . . . Ζωή ist im Johannesevangelium nicht das von der Schöpfung her in den Menschen oder gar in der Welt überhaupt schon vorhandene, sondern das in der Erlösung herbeikommende, dem Menschen irgendwie erst zu schenkende, durchaus supranaturale *neue* Leben. Sollte es wirklich erlaubt sein, anzunehmen, dass gerade an unserer Stelle eine Ausnahme stattfinden und das natürliche, allen Kreaturen als solchen von Gott verliehene Leben gemeint sein sollte? Ist es nicht wahrscheinlicher, dass der Begriff gerade an unserer Stelle, wo er zum ersten Mal auftritt, prägnant, d.h. im Sinn des ganzen übrigen Evangeliums gebraucht sein muss?

Und ganz ebenso steht es nun . . . mit dem subordinierten Begriff φῶς. Ich möchte einmal die Stelle sehen im Johannesevangelium, wo "Licht" ein von der Schöpfung her schon vorhandenes, in und mit dem Schöpfungsleben gegebenes, als ungeschaffenes Licht der geschaffenen Welt einfach präsentes und nicht vielmehr das mit dem Erlösungsleben erst kommende—gewiss vielleicht schon von Uranfang her kommende, aber eben wirklich *kommende—Offenbarungs*licht wäre.

all of them together can outweigh the considerations which we have just developed and which are in themselves decisive.[84]

(iv) We come finally to what we have called the *"imago Dei"* interpretation of John 1:4a (*Reading II*). As pointed out early on, the most important study ever done on John 1:3/4 was that of Aland, "Eine Untersuchung zu Joh. 1:3-4: Über die Bedeutung eines Punktes," a study which we have cited repeatedly. Aland's work on John 1:3/4 is concerned almost entirely with the textual question, with respect to which he argues emphatically and exhaustively for *Reading II*. He does, however, in the concluding pages of his study venture an interpretation of *Reading II*,[85] still different from those we have already encountered.

Aland, like these others, adopts *Reading II-B*. His reasoning is that the exclusive force of χωρὶς αὐτοῦ ἐγένετο οὐδὲ ἕν in vs. 3 would either trivialize or make impossible the inclusive ὃ γέγονεν ἐν αὐτῷ, ζωὴ ἦν, that is, *Reading II-A*. Having announced that *without* the Logos, apart from the Logos, nothing can have come into being, the Evangelist could not then immediately announce further that what has come into being *in* the Logos, was life. It accords, rather, with the whole message of John (so Aland) that in-him-was-life. Thus, *Reading II-B*. Further, as was mentioned already, Aland takes it as self-evident that ζωή must mean here what it means everywhere else in John, namely, spiritual life. He takes it, though, as referring to the spiritual life of man as originally created by God, life before the Fall:

> Vv. 1-4 schildern die Zeit und den Zustand vor und bei der Erschaffung der Welt. Die Menschen jener Zeit besassen ζωή und φῶς—bis zum Sündenfall; den sie waren in dem Zustand, der durch die Sendung des fleischgewordenen Logos für die gefallene Menschheit wiederhergestellt werden soll. Mit v. 4 ist die Bezugnahme auf die Urgeschichte abgeschlossen, in vs. 5 wird mit einem Satz die Situation der Welt nach dem Sündenfall charakterisiert, mit vs. 6 wird dann sofort die dritte Epoche angesprochen, die mit der Fleischwerdung des Logos angebrochen ist.[86]

---

[84] The general situation with respect to the interpretation of "life" and "light" in John 1:4 is typified by Morris who grants that "'life' in John characteristically refers to eternal life," but then immediately declares that in 1:4 "the term must be taken in its broadest sense" (*The Gospel according to John*, p. 82). But what, especially in view of Morris' first statement, is the justification of the "must" in the second? Surely the most natural procedure would be first to exhaust the possibility that "life" in vs. 4 also refers to eternal life. As we shall see, this possibility is exactly what virtually all commentators fail to attend to.

[85] Almost, it seems, apologetically: ". . . es [ist] nicht die Absicht dieser Studie, in das Geschäft der Exegeten einzugreifen. . . ."; "Aber das sind nur Vorschläge der Textkritik an die Adresse der Exegeten" ("Eine Untersuchung zu Joh. 1:3-4," pp. 204f., 209).

[86] Aland, "Eine Untersuchung zu Joh. 1:3-4," p. 207. While Hartwig Thyen is absolutely correct in his impression when he says, "Mir scheint . . . undenkbar, dass im JohEv die blosse biologische Lebendigkeit je 'Leben' heissen kann" ("Aus der Literatur zum Johannesevangelium," *TR*, 39 (1975), p. 62, n. 3), he is therefore wrong in attributing this erroneous view to Aland.

This interpretation of the first verses of John leads Aland to what he regards the inevitable translation of vs. 4a: "Was geworden ist, war in ihm Leben."

How is ὃ γέγονεν understood on this rendering? From a linguistic standpoint, Aland answers that "das Perfect ὃ γέγονεν versteht sich aus der Fortdauer der Schöpfung von einst. . . ."[87] From the standpoint of its meaning, ὃ γέγονεν, especially in view of vs. 4b, καὶ ἡ ζωὴ ἦν τὸ φῶς τῶν ἀνθρώπων, appears to apply specifically to men. This restriction of ὃ γέγονεν to mankind is defended by Aland on the grounds that in John 1:1-5 the lines connected with preceding lines by καί all have the same reference as the preceding line, and vs. 4b "redet nur von den Menschen." In contrast with vs. 3, then, vs. 4 narrows our attention from creation in general to mankind, which, after all, is what the rest of the Prologue is really concerned with—the activity of the Logos, vis à vis man.[88]

As with the other interpretations, Aland's involves *Reading II-B*, and, like the others, it construes ὃ γέγονεν as referring to something created, in this case mankind, a narrowing of the πάντα of vs. 3. Enough has already been said about the problems with *Reading II-B* except to add that the incompatibility which Aland sees between the exclusive χωρίς of vs. 3 and the inclusive ἐν of vs. 4 may strike one as being somewhat heavy-handed, and, in any case, if the ἐν of vs. 4 could be interpreted instrumentally (which is at least possible), why could it not be compatible with the instrumental διά of vs. 3 as easily as it is incompatible with the χωρίς of vs. 3? Next is the matter of Aland's restriction of ὃ γέγονεν to mankind. Specifically, while there is something to Aland's claim about the pattern of lines connected by καί (recall the staircase parallelisms that character-ize John 1:1-5), it is not the case that vs. 4b "redet nur von Menschen." Why could not the common reference between vs. 4b and the preceding vs. 4a just as easily be ζωή as ἄνθρωπος? At least in that case the reference in both lines would be identical and unambiguous, something that could hardly be claimed for ὃ γέγονεν = ἄνθρωποι! More generally, Aland's observation about ὃ γέγονεν as designating the continuity of creation from once upon a time and his limitation of ὃ γέγονεν to mankind (at least primarily) are, from an exegetical standpoint, subtle beyond what one might reasonably expect from the author of these lines.

Most important is Aland's interpretation of ὃ γέγονεν as referring to something created, in this case mankind. We have already seen that in fact *all* of the usual interpretations of ὃ γέγονεν construe it as referring to

---

[87] Aland, "Eine Untersuchung zu Joh. 1:3-4," p. 207.
[88] Aland, "Eine Untersuchung zu Joh. 1:3-4," p. 209.

something created, and it will be necessary to challenge these interpretations at this their most crucial point. For the moment, however, yet another matter must be addressed:

The Πάντα of Verse 3 Reconsidered

We have considered four ways in which John 1:4, according to *Reading II*, has been interpreted: the metaphysical, existential, naturalistic, and *imago Dei* interpretations. (We devoted more space to the naturalistic interpretation of our passage, not only because this interpretation has been, in various ways, the most pervasive, but because the discussion bears at many points on issues to be raised again.) Setting aside the ancient heretical views, virtually all commentators on this text, both ancient and modern, have decided on one or the other of these interpretations, though we have seen that there may be variations on a theme. Our conclusion is that each of these four main lines of interpretation must be rejected for various reasons.

But it is important now to see that the assumption that lies behind most attempts to make sense of John 1:4 (*Reading II*)—ancient and modern, heretical and orthodox—is that ὃ γέγονεν in 1:4a must refer in some way or other to something created. In the four representative interpretations considered above this is, specifically, the general or natural creation already mentioned in vs. 3. Excluding the Philonic "spekulative Gedanke," we have seen that on the metaphysical interpretation of Augustine *et al.*, ὃ γέγονεν in vs. 4a takes up the πάντα, or creation, of vs. 3 and now relates it to Life, the Divine Reason, as the cause of its intelligibility; on the existential interpretation of Bultmann, ὃ γέγονεν in vs. 4a refers to πάντα, or natural creation, in vs. 3, but focuses now on the revelatory-existential character of creation; on the naturalistic interpretation of Boismard *et al.*, ὃ γέγονεν in vs. 4a restates the πάντα of vs. 3, though introducing now the themes of life and light understood as special features of natural creation; on Aland's *imago Dei* interpretation, ὃ γέγονεν etc. in vs. 4 refers primarily to pre-fallen man and thus is a refinement or restriction of the more inclusive πάντα in vs. 3. But the failure of these interpretations suggests that if we too hold to the view that ὃ γέγονεν in vs. 4a represents an extension or restatement in different terms of the πάντα of vs. 3, then what may be called for is a radical reconsideration of the πάντα.

If we take πάντα in vs. 3 not as referring to natural creation after all, to what, then, does it refer? Three possibilities present themselves, all of them unacceptable. Attention has already been called to the Gnostic interpretations of the first verses of John. Specifically on vs. 3 it was common for Gnostics, such as the Valentinian Ptolemaeus, to refer the πάντα or "all things" brought into being through the Logos to the primal αἰών or the πλήρωμα.[89] We have noted too the Philonic interpretation (the "spckulative Gedanke") according to which the πάντα, all things created through the Logos, in vs. 3 refers to the transcendent and archetypal world in the Divine Mind.[90] Whatever historical interest such views may hold, they are irrelevant here; they assume a philosophical-theological frame of reference which is hardly appropriate for the first verses of John.

A third possibility, advanced by Pollard, requires more attention. Pollard argues that the πάντα of John 1:3 refers not to the natural creation but to the wider domain of all of God's revelatory and redemptive acts:

> The πάντα . . . refers to the relationship of God with mankind in His self-revelation, and this interpretation of the word agrees with the message of the Gospel as a whole: through his words and deeds, by which he reveals the Father to men and redeems them, the Son is the mediator of "all" things that God does and says.[91]

As hinted in this quotation, Pollard's main argument against the usual and narrower view that John 1:3 refers to God's creation of the world through the Logos is that the central theme of the Fourth Gospel as a whole is not cosmology but rather God's saving activity in Christ, and "it is not unreasonable to expect that this would also be the main theme of the Prologue."[92] He buttresses this primary line of argument with some secondary considerations. If John had intended to speak here of creation he would have employed τὸ πᾶν or τὰ πάντα; πάντα, says Pollard, suggests something wider, especially here where (on *Reading II*) it is defined more closely in vs. 4 as ζωή, which certainly encompasses something more, and more salvific, than creation. This "general" meaning of πάντα suggests in turn a more general meaning for the verb ἐγένετο, something like "happened," rather than the specific "were made," and this "general" meaning of γίνομαι is perfectly possible.[93]

Surely Pollard is correct in his view that the central theme of the whole Fourth Gospel is God's revealing and redeeming acts in Christ, and he rightly justifies this with an appeal to John's stated purpose in 20:31 as well as to the soteriological concerns which pervade the whole Gospel. He is also correct in his judgment that the central theme of John's Gospel should coincide with the central theme of the Prologue. His error appears

---

[89] Cf. Pagels, *The Johannine Gospel in Gnostic Exegesis*, Ch. 1.
[90] See above in the discussion of the "metaphysical" interpretation of *Reading II*.
[91] T. Evan Pollard, "Cosmology and the Prologue of the Fourth Gospel," *VC*, 12 (1958), p. 150.
[92] Pollard, "Cosmology and the Prologue of the Fourth Gospel," p. 149.
[93] Pollard, "Cosmology and the Prologue of the Fourth Gospel," pp. 149ff.

to be a simple logical one: Since no one is claiming that the reference to creation in John 1:3 is the *central* theme of anything at all, Pollard's entire effort is misplaced. Further, while there is no *a priori* reason to exclude cosmological interest entirely from the Fourth Gospel, there are good reasons for retaining the cosmological interpretation of John 1:3. First, though we do not go as far as some in insisting on parallels between the first verses of John and the first verses of Genesis, it is hardly possible to deny them utterly; especially in view of the fact that John's first words, ἐν ἀρχῇ, coincide exactly with the first words of the Septuagint, it would be strange not to see in vs. 3 a reference to the creation of the world. Second, we do find as straightforward a cosmological reference as one could hope for in vs. 10b, ὁ κόσμος δι' αὐτοῦ ἐγένετο, and it would be exceedingly odd if the almost identical expression in vs. 3a, πάντα δι' αὐτοῦ ἐγένετο, meant something very different. If indeed the claim in vs. 10b is parallel to that in vs. 3a, then πάντα in vs. 3a means the created world (κόσμος in vs. 10b), and this is sufficient evidence against Pollard's supporting argument that πάντα means something wider and different than τὸ πᾶν or τὰ πάντα. It is true that τὸ πᾶν or τὰ πάντα would be more appropriate than πάντα as a designation for the world. But in view of the parallelism between vss. 3a and 10b a cosmological reference in vs. 3a is undeniable and the most that might be granted with respect to πάντα in vs. 3 rather than τὰ πάντα is that the former refers, as Morris suggests, to "all things taken individually rather than to the universe as a totality."[94] Finally, Pollard's "more accurate" translation of vs. 3a, "Everything happens through Him,"[95] fails utterly to do justice to the aorist ἐγένετο. Whatever is in view here, it is properly represented as past and punctiliar, exactly as with the parallel ἐγένετο of vs. 10b, not to mention three others in the Prologue, vss. 6, 14, and 17.

Pollard's wider and soteriological interpretation of the πάντα of vs. 3 was subsequently embraced by Lamarche who, like Pollard, stressed the more general meaning of ἐγένετο ("happened"),[96] and also by de la Potterie who recapitulated Pollard's argument from the general meaning of ἐγένετο and the argument from πάντα vs. τὸ πᾶν, but added some supporting considerations of his own. First, he appeals to the prepositional phrase δι' αὐτοῦ, which he calls "la formule centrale du v. 3a," as peculiarly suited in John to Jesus' mediation of salvation (as in 3:17), and thus as yielding a soteriological meaning for πάντα.[97] Also, and to the challenge

[94] Morris, *The Gospel according to John*, p. 79, n. 20.
[95] Pollard, "Cosmology and the Prologue of the Fourth Gospel," p. 152.
[96] Lamarche, "Le Prologue de Jean," pp. 524ff.
[97] Ignace de la Potterie, *La Vérité dans Saint Jean* (Rome: Biblical Institute Press, 1977), II, p. 164.

that vs. 3 is parallel to the clearly cosmological idea in vs. 10, he argues that though κόσμος in John surely does at times signify the world (as in 11:9; 17:5, 24; 21:25), more often it signifies the domain of humanity (as in 3:19; 4:42; 8:12; 16:8), and more specifically the domain of a rejecting and disbelieving humanity (as in 7:7; 12:3; 15:18-19). For de la Potterie, vs. 10c, with its identification of κόσμος with the domain of uncomprehending humanity, controls the meaning for κόσμος in vs. 10b also and thus the latter cannot be the created world nor can ἐγένετο here be rendered "was made." The upshot is that vs. 10b is not a cosmological statement to start with, and therefore cannot dictate a cosmological interpretation of the allegedly parallel vs. 3.[98]

Enough has already been said about the arguments based on the meaning of ἐγένετο and on πάντα vs. τὸ πᾶν. With respect to de la Potterie's appeal to the soteriological significance of δι' αὐτοῦ: The phrase itself is, of course, very natural and is used in a great variety of contexts in John, and it seems to us to be a case of special pleading to insist on a soteriological significance of vs. 3. On the other hand, there is a contextual consideration: He thinks, especially on the basis of *Reading I*, that the meaning of vs. 3 is to be interpreted in view of soteriological content of vs. 4.[99] This fails, however, to reckon with the shift (significant, we will argue later) from the aorist ἐγένετο in vs. 3 to the perfect γέγονεν in vs. 4, and from the δι' αὐτοῦ in vs. 3 to the ἐν αὐτῷ in vs. 4. With respect to de la Potterie's rejection of the cosmological intent of vs. 10b and thus also of the similar sounding vs. 3: He rightly notes the fluid meaning of κόσμος in John, but this is precisely what weighs against his view of κόσμος in vs. 10b. The fluidity is no more evident than in vs. 10 where, on our interpretation, we encounter κόσμος in the larger sense of the created order (vs. 10b) which is then narrowed to designate the domain of unbelieving men (vs. 10c). This is exactly what happens in the immediately following (!) vs. 11 which we take to be loosely parallel in meaning to vs. 10: "He came to his own (τὰ ἴδια), and his own (οἱ ἴδιοι) did not accept him." Here we have a similar narrowing from τὰ ἴδια, which we take to designate the whole created order, to οἱ ἴδιοι, which we take to designate the sphere of humanity.[100]

---

[98] De la Potterie, *La Vérité dans Saint Jean*, II, pp. 164f.

[99] De la Potterie, *La Vérité dans Saint Jean*, II, p. 163.

[100] With his maverick view that, specifically, vss. 3-4 together speak of the historical advent of salvific life and light—the incarnation—de la Potterie moves beyond the naturalistic interpretation of vs. 4 (*Reading II*) he espoused in 1955 (see above, p. 62), in the direction of what we will call the incarnational interpretation. We will see, though, that on our view the cosmological interpretation of the πάντα of vs. 3 (which de la Potterie so ardently rejects) fits perfectly with the contrasting soteriological thrust of vs. 4 (which he so ardently affirms).

In agreement, then, with virtually all commentators on John 1:3, we take πάντα there to refer to the natural world created by God through the instrumentality of the Logos, and we reject all attempts that we have encountered to interpret it otherwise. It is somewhat ironical, though, that we could not agree more with Pollard when he says,

> . . . John wrote his Prologue as a summary of the *Heilsgeschichte* of which the incarnate life of the Son of God is the central point, and . . . it is as such that he intended the Prologue to be read.[101]

The interpretation of πάντα in John 1:3 as designating the created world is not an alien intrusion into the *Heilsgeschichte* of John's Prologue, but, on the contrary, contributes to it a decisive element.

Reading II: *The Incarnational Interpretation*

We come now to an important transition in our present discussion. To this point our analysis has been on the whole negative, that is, critical of the various attempts to make sense of John 1:4 on *Reading II*. On the other hand, it has been hinted all along that there is open to us yet another and altogether different interpretation of the passage. This more constructive part of our discussion will involve a radical reinterpretation not of the πάντα of vs. 3, but rather of the ὃ γέγονεν of vs. 4. We shall propose an alternate and *un*problematic meaning for ὃ γέγονεν, and contend later that this new meaning of ὃ γέγονεν is a key to the logical/theological structure of the hymnic lines in John 1:1-5. More specifically, we have seen that John 1:4 (*Reading II*) is problematic so long as ὃ γέγονεν is thought to refer to something created, or more often, is regarded as an extension, a continuation, or restatement of the πάντα (= creation) of vs. 3. We wish now to argue that ὃ γέγονεν in vs. 4 has, in fact, no reference whatsoever to anything created, much less to the πάντα of vs. 3, and that it introduces an entirely new thought, one that makes good theological and Johannine sense.

Surely Brown represents a new direction from those we have just encountered when he rejects ὃ γέγονεν = πάντα, opts for *Reading II-A*, and insists that ζωή must here refer to the eternal life which is in the Son. Nonetheless, says Brown, the passage refers to the creation account of Genesis where

> that which had especially come to be in God's creative Word was the gift of eternal life. This life was the light of men because the tree of life was

---

[101] Pollard, "Cosmology and the Prologue of the Fourth Gospel," p. 149.

closely associated with the tree of the knowledge of good and evil. If man had survived the test, he would have possessed eternal life and enlightenment.[102]

For justification of this interpretation he appeals not only to the tree of life whose fruit grants eternal life (Gen. 2:9 and 3:22), but also to the way in which, according to Rev. 22:2, this life prefigures the life that Jesus brings, and to the bread of life in John 6 which answers to the tree of life in Paradise, and to John 8:44 with its echo of the serpent's lie to Eve and man's consequent loss of the opportunity of eternal life.[103] Thus Brown's rendering of John 1:4a (*Reading II*): "That which had come to be in him was life."[104] And vs. 5 turns out to be a reference to the Fall, and involves an echo of Gen. 3:15 in that the seed of the woman, Jesus, would be victorious over Satan.[105]

While we think that Brown is correct in adopting *Reading II-A* and insisting that ζωή must here mean eternal, not natural, life, Brown's employment of Rev. 22:2, John 6, and John 8:44 may strike one as forced. Still, there is merit to this interpretation. In fact, if the interpretation that we ourselves shall propose is false, then this one, or something close to it, must be true. But it is incompatible with the view to be developed below and in our final chapter, and one will have to weigh its strengths against any merit one finds in our subsequent points.

Stated as explicitly as possible, our view is that John 1:4 is to be read in accordance with *Reading II-A*, ὃ γέγονεν ἐν αὐτῷ, ζωὴ ἦν, καὶ ἡ ζωὴ ἦν τὸ φῶς τῶν ἀνθρώπων, that it is to be translated something like, "That which appeared in him was life, and the life was the light of men," and that it expresses the Johannine belief that salvific life and light has appeared to men in the historical advent of the incarnate Logos. In John 1:4 we have, therefore, the first reference in the Prologue, and thus in the Gospel of John, to the Incarnation. Even though we shall argue that this interpretation of John 1:4 (*Reading II*) is the most natural and simple, it has seldom been advanced, and nowhere systematically or exhaustively.[106] In the tradition, the incarnational interpretation was

---

[102] Brown, *The Gospel according to John*, I, p. 27.

[103] Brown, *The Gospel according to John*, I, p. 27.

[104] Brown, *The Gospel according to John*, I, p. 3.

[105] Brown, *The Gospel according to John*, I, p. 27.

[106] From the word "new" in the title of my article, "The Logic of the Logos Hymn: A New View," Rochais has accused me of ignorance of the fact that the incarnational interpretation of John 1:4a (*Reading II*) has had earlier advocates ("La Formation du Prologue (Jn. 1:1-18)," p. 14, n. 13). However, what I presented there as new was the view that vss. 1-5 contained a complete, four-strophe, salvation-historical hymn (see below, Ch. III). On the other hand, Fredric Schlatter grossly overstates the case when he says that "most critics who accept [*Reading II* of John 1:3/4] see in the text a reference to the incarnation" ("The Problem of Jn. 1:3b-4a" p. 54).

variously advanced by Origen, St. Hilary, and St. Ambrose.[107] It was, indeed, given eloquent expression by St. Ambrose who linked John 1:4a (*Reading II*) with I John 1:1-2 and then makes his interpretation of the former as clear as one could hope for—ὃ γέγονεν signifies the whole historical and salvific drama of the incarnate Logos:

> "Quod factum est in ipso, vita est." . . . "Quod erat ab initio, et quod audivimus, et vidimus oculis nostris, quod perspeximus, et manus nostrae scrutatae sunt de Verbo vitae, et vita apparuit." Caro ergo est quae in Christo apparuit, vel Christus in carne; ipse nostra in omnibus vita est. Ipsius divinitas, vita est; ipsius aeternitas, vita est; ipsius caro, vita est; ipsius passio, vita est. . . . Umbra alarum, umbra crucis, umbra est passionis. Ipsius mors, vita est; ipsius vulnus, vita est; ipsius sanguis, vita est; ipsius sepultura, vita est; ipsius resurrectio, vita est universorum.[108]

Modern proponents of the incarnational interpretation include, in various ways, Lacan, Vawter, Lamarche, and F. Schlatter.[109]

Our own defense of the incarnational interpretation of John 1:4 (*Reading II*) takes both a negative and positive form.

On the negative side, we should find ourselves at least open to the incarnational interpretation of John 1:4 (*Reading II*) in view of the failure of all other attempts to provide a good sense for the passage. This failure has to some degree been aided and abetted by the adoption of *Reading II-B*. Though our inclination has been to reject this reading on grammatical/stylistic grounds, we will see later that the issue of *Reading II-A* vs. *Reading II-B* turns out not to be a decisive one. What is important is the way the metaphysical, naturalistic and *imago Dei* interpretations construe ὃ γέγονεν as referring to creation, that is, as an extension of the πάντα of vs. 3. We have seen that this, along with other problems involved in these interpretations, turn these interpretations into dead ends. And we have seen also that the attempt to reinterpret the πάντα of vs. 3 along more soteriological than cosmological lines fails too. Apart from abandoning *Reading II* for *Reading I* (a desperate solution) the failure of these attempted resolutions of the *lectio difficilior* press one, I say, toward a more

---

[107] Origen, *In Ioannis Evangelium*, II, 12 (*PG*, 14, 147); St. Hilary, *De Trinitate*, II, 20 (*PL*, 10, 63); St. Ambrose, *In Psalmum*, XXXVI, 36 (*PL*, 14, 1031).

[108] St. Ambrose, *In Psalmum*, XXXVI, 36 (*PL*, 14, 1031).

[109] M.-F. Lacan, "L'Oeuvre du Verbe Incarné," pp. 61ff.; Vawter, "What Came to Be in Him Was Life (Jn. 1:3b-4a)," pp. 401ff.; Paul Lamarche, "Le Prologue de Jean," pp. 523ff.; F. Schlatter, "The Problem of John 1:3b-4a," pp. 54ff. Loisy may be mentioned too, though his interpretation involves a significant variation. He strongly emphasized ζωή and φῶς as references to the incarnation, but adopted *Reading II-B* and understood ὃ γέγονεν to refer to the created world of men in which the incarnate life and light appeared. According to Loisy, the meaning of the passage: "That which has come to be, namely, the world of men, in it was the life of the incarnate Logos, and this life was the light of men" (*Le Quatrième Évangele*, pp. 92ff.).

radical approach to the passage, namely, a radically different interpretation of the ὃ γέγονεν of vs. 4.

So much for the negative side of our defense. The positive evidence for the incarnational interpretation of John 1:4 (*Reading II*) proceeds along six lines.

(i) We have seen repeatedly that most commentators on John 1:4 (*Reading II*), ancient and modern, have understood ὃ γέγονεν as designating something created, usually the natural creation referred to already by the πάντα in vs. 3. In English translation it usually turns up as "that which has been made," as in the *Revised Standard Version* (in a note indicating the alternate *Reading II*), and most translations and commentators render it similarly: "what was made," "quod factum est," "was gemacht ist," and the like.

But it should be noted that such translations of ὃ γέγονεν in vs. 4 as "that which has been made," and of πάντα ἐγένετο in vs. 3 as "all things were made," strictly do violence to the expressions inasmuch as they turn what is an intransitive verb in Greek, γίνομαι, into a transitive verb in translation—even the lexicons are misleading here, as when Bauer gives "to be made, created," as a meaning of the deponent γίνομαι.[110] This point, which may appear to be somewhat academic, does in fact bear upon our argument, for the translation "that which has been made" for ὃ γέγονεν almost certainly tilts the interpretation of the phrase in the direction of creation (what else could "that which has been made" in vs. 4 refer to other than to the created world just previously mentioned in vs. 3?) whereas the translation "that which has come into being" is clearly open to other interpretations, as we shall see. It is important now to appreciate that while the verb γίνομαι bears a kind of ontological-existential signification ("to be," "to become," "to come into being"), it also bears a historical-temporal signification ("to come to pass," "come on the scene," "appear," "happen," "occur," "arise," and so forth).[111] And it does not follow from the fact that the ἐγένετο in vs. 3 bears the first of these meanings that γέγονεν in vs. 4 must also. That γέγονεν in vs. 4 might very well not bear the first of these meanings, and might in fact bear the second, is suggested by the following.

As throughout the New Testament, John also frequently employs ἐγένετο with the common meaning "it came to pass," more idiomatically

---

[110] Walter Bauer, *A Greek-English Lexicon of the New Testament and Other Early Christian Literature*, tr. William F. Arndt and F. Wilbur Gringrich, second ed., ed. F. Wilbur Gingrich and Frederick W. Danker (Chicago: University of Chicago Press, 1979), "γίνομαι," I, 2.

[111] Cf. Bauer, *A Greek-English Lexicon of the New Testament and Other Early Christian Literature*, "γίνομαι," I, 1, b.

translated as "it happened," "it occurred," and the like, as in John 1:28
("These things *happened* beyond the Jordan"), 2:1 ("And on the third day
a wedding *took place* in Cana"), 3:25 ("There *arose* a discussion between
John's disciples and a Jew"), and numerous similar instances. More
significantly, at 5:14 John alternates between the ontological-existential
and the historical-temporal meanings of γίνομαι in the same verse
("Look, you have become (γέγονας) well: Sin no more, lest something
worse happen (γένηται) to you!"). And in the Prologue itself, John passes
from the ontological meaning of ἐγένετο in vs. 3 ("All things came into
being (ἐγένετο) through him, and apart from him came into being
(ἐγένετο) nothing") (note also vs. 10) to the historical meaning in vs. 6
("There appeared (ἐγένετο) a man sent from God, whose name was
John") and again in vs. 17 ("grace and truth appeared (ἐγένετο) through
Jesus Christ").[112] With respect to the perfect form γέγονεν specifically,
John uses this here and there throughout his Gospel with the historical-
temporal meaning as in 12:30 ("Not for my sake has this voice come
(γέγονεν), but for your sake"), 14:22 ("Master, what has happened (τί
γέγονεν) that you are about to reveal yourself to us, but not to the world?"),
and in the second person 6:25 ("Rabbi, when did you come (γέγονας)
here?"). It is to be noted, too, that the exact phrase ὃ γέγονεν otherwise
occurs in the New Testament only in Mark 5:33 where it means necessarily "what has happened."

Thus the possibility, at least, must be entertained that in John 1:4
γέγονεν signifies the historical advent of spiritual life in the Logos: What
has come about, happened, appeared, arrived, etc. in him was life. The
probability that this is the meaning of the passage is not a little
strengthened when it is compared to other passages in John where life or
light are bound up with the idea of the Logos' advent. For example:

And this is the judgment, that the light has come into the world. . . .
(John 3:19).

. . . the bread of God is that which comes down from heaven and gives
life to the world (John 6:33).

As long as I am in the world I am the light of the world (John 9:5).

I have come as a light into the world, that whoever believes in me may
not remain in darkness (John 12:46).

---

[112] We do not insist on this interpretation of the ἐγένετο in John 1:17, but it is supported
by the *parallelismus* in the complete verse and also by the nature of grace and truth (i.e.
grace and truth did not themselves come into existence with Jesus Christ).

. . . the life was made visible, and we have seen and witness and proclaim to you the eternal life which was with the Father and was made visible to us. . . . (I John 1:2).

It is a pervasive Johannine theme that spiritual and salvific life and light has appeared, come on the scene, been revealed in the incarnate Logos. The incarnational interpretation of John 1:4 is in itself neither grammatically nor theologically unnatural, and it coheres with this major and recurring Johannine idea.

(ii) John employs the verb γίνομαι nine times and in three different forms in the Prologue as we have it: the aorist tense ἐγένετο in vss. 3 (twice), 6, 10, 14, and 17; the perfect tense γέγονεν in vss. 3 and 15; the infinitive γενέσθαι in vs. 13. This usage is not haphazard or arbitrary. In every instance of the aorist ἐγένετο in the Prologue a definite point in past time is indicated: when the world came into being (vs. 3), when John the Baptist appeared (vs. 6), when the Logos became flesh (vs. 14), when grace and truth appeared through Jesus Christ (vs. 17). There is nothing surprising in this, for the usual function of the aorist tense is to denote a simple or punctiliar action in the past, an action that occurred "once upon a time." The perfect tense, however, is more of a present than a past tense in that it emphasizes the present and continuing consequences of a past action.[113] And since John in particular is attentive to his use of the perfect,[114] it is hard to accept that if John intended the relative clause of vs. 4a to restate the πάντα ἐγένετο of vs. 3 he would not have used the same aorist form, ὃ ἐγένετο.[115] As it is, the perfect γέγονεν in vs. 4a stands in unmistakable contrast to the two instances of the aorist ἐγένετο in vs.

---

[113] On the distinction between the aorist and the perfect tenses in the New Testament in general, see Maximilian Zerwick, *Biblical Greek*, fourth ed., tr. and rev. Joseph Smith (Rome: Pontifical Biblical Institute, 1963), sects. 285ff. Also Blass/Debrunner, *A Greek Grammar of the New Testament and Other Early Christian Literature*, sects. 340, 342.

[114] Cf. Bruce M. Metzger, "The Language of the New Testament," *The Interpreter's Bible* (New York: Abingdon Press, 1951), VII, pp. 50f. Though Metzger takes an altogether different view of the passage, relevant here is his comment on John's use of the perfect tense: "The reader of the Greek text soon discovers that John is particularly fond of the perfect tense. As compared with the Synoptic Gospels, John uses the perfect (and pluperfect) tense three times as often as Mark and Luke do, and five times as often as Matthew does; furthermore, I John uses it twice as often, proportionately to length, as does the Fourth Gospel. John's overworking of the perfect tense is probably to be explained by his wish to emphasize thereby the abiding consequences and eternal significance of the work and words of God's only Son."

[115] Vawter, who accepts *Reading II-A* and the incarnational interpretation, applies the issue of the perfect tense directly to our passage: "The evidence of the NT is that its authors, including Jn, have preserved the sense of the Greek perfect and have not confounded it with the aorist. Thus ὃ γέγονεν could hardly refer to created being as continually coming into existence throughout time." ("What Came to Be in Him was Life (Jn. 1:3b-4a)," p. 404).

3.[116] That there is reflected in the Prologue a real difference between the aorist and the perfect forms of γίνομαι is further supported by the fact that on the second instance of the perfect γέγονεν, in vs. 15, the thought clearly excludes the past and punctiliar idea of the aorist ἐγένετο; the thought is, rather, that the Logos was and *continues to be* superior to the Baptist.

We conclude that the shift from the aorist ἐγένετο (twice) in vs. 3 to the perfect γέγονεν in vs. 4a probably signals the introduction of a new thought. We have already expressed our view that the perfect clause of John 1:4a introduces the incarnation.

(iii) We must also take account of the change from the prepositional phrase δι' αὐτοῦ in vs. 3 to ἐν αὐτῷ in vs. 4. If John had intended by ὃ γέγονεν ἐν αὐτῷ in vs. 4 to recall the πάντα δι' αὐτοῦ ἐγένετο in vs. 3, he could have more naturally used not only the same verb form, ἐγένετο, but also the same prepositional phrase, δι' αὐτοῦ. As it is, we are made to wonder whether there is some significance in the change to the prepositional phrase ἐν αὐτῷ. If one reads the passage according to *Reading II-B*, ὃ γέγονεν, ἐν αὐτῷ ζωὴ ἦν, then the change to ἐν αὐτῷ could make a certain sense for it would then express something quite different from the δι' αὐτοῦ in vs. 3—not the instrumentality of creation but the how and why of creation's relation to life. But this view must face the point raised repeatedly that *Reading II-B* involves an anacoluthon (*casus pendens*) which, though certainly found elsewhere in John, probably should be rejected if the non-anacoluthic *Reading II-A* can be accepted, and we are in the process of showing that it can be. Also, this view will now have to square itself with the demonstration that ζωή in John always means spiritual and salvific life—unless one wants to claim that all of nature was from the start possessed of salvific life. On the other hand, if one reads the passage according to *Reading II-A*, ὃ γέγονεν ἐν αὐτῷ, ζωὴ ἦν, and takes ὃ γέγονεν ἐν αὐτῷ as a restatement of πάντα δι' αὐτοῦ ἐγένετο in vs. 3, then the ἐν, like the διά, must be instrumental. This too is problematic. In the Fourth Gospel ἐν occurs innumerable times but with the instrumental sense only rarely. The case against an instrumental ἐν at John 1:4 is even tighter if we restrict our attention to the Prologue. The preposition διά with the genitive occurs five times in the Prologue and always, as we would expect, with the instrumental meaning of "through"; the preposition ἐν occurs five times, in addition to the instance in vs. 4, and never with the

---

[116] Even Zahn, who took the relative clause ὃ γέγονεν as concluding vs. 3 (i.e. *Reading I*), felt it necessary to reckon with the different tenses in that verse: "Das Perf. γέγονεν, welches nach dem zweimaligen ἐγένετο um so mehr ins Ohr fällt, versetzt den Leser in die Gegenwart und bezeichnet das in der Gegenwart Existirende als das fertige Produkt des vollendeten Werdens" (*Das Evangelium des Johannes*, p. 52). ὃ γέγονεν is here conspicuous by its presence.

instrumental meaning. This, plus the immediate proximity of the διά in vs. 3, weighs heavily against the likelihood of an instrumental sense of ἐν suddenly intruding at vs. 4.

Our conclusion here is similar to the one drawn above on the basis of the contrast between the aorist tense ἐγένετο in vs. 3 and the perfect tense γέγονεν in vs. 4: The phrase ἐν αὐτῷ in vs. 4, standing in stark contrast to the δι' αὐτοῦ in vs. 3, is probably an indication that with the first line of vs. 4 we pass to a new idea. And, again, what the new idea is may be suggested by other passages in John where spiritual life and light are represented as "in" the Logos or where he is otherwise represented as the *locus* of life and light. For example:

> For as the Father has life in himself so he has granted the Son also to have life in himself (John 5:26).

> . . . you refuse to come to me that you may have life (John 5:40).

> I am the light of the world (John 8:12).

> I am the way, and the truth, and the life (John 14:6).

> . . . this is the testimony, that God gave us eternal life, and this life is in his Son (I John 5:11).

(iv) Still another indication that the scene changes between John 1:3 and 1:4 (*Reading II*) is the reference in 1:4 to "men." Our focus is thus narrowed from the whole of creation in vs. 3 to the restricted sphere of men in vs. 4. This is all the more significant since it is not just men that are in view here, but men in relation to life and light, and the salvific character of this life and light was demonstrated earlier. The shift, then, from vs. 3 to vs. 4 does not involve simply a shift from the thought of creation as a whole to the special sphere of men in particular, but a shift from the idea of creation to the idea of salvation. The phrase πάντα δι' αὐτοῦ ἐγένετο in vs. 3 asserts, on this understanding, that all things came into being through the Logos, whereas ὃ γέγονεν ἐν αὐτῷ ζωὴ ἦν, καὶ ἡ ζωὴ ἦν τὸ φῶς τῶν ἀνθρώπων in vs. 4 asserts that eschatological life and light has appeared for men in the Logos.

It should be noted too that the same contrast and movement of ideas that we find in vss. 3-4, bearing first on the creation of the world and then on the salvation of men, is similar to what we find in vss. 10-11 where the thought passes (though not in logical sequence) from the creation of the world through the Logos to his incarnate presence in the world and the rejection of him by the world of men: "He was in the world, and the world came into being through him, and yet the world did not recognize him.

He came to his own, yet his own people did not accept him." Such a comparison of vss. 3-4 (*Reading II*) and vss. 10-11 suggests that the connection and contrast of creation and incarnation may be, in the Prologue material, something of a pattern.[117] The suggestion is strengthened by the phrase ὁ κόσμος δι' αὐτοῦ ἐγένετο in vs. 10, virtually identical to the πάντα δι' αὐτοῦ ἐγένετο in vs. 3. And could not the phrases ἐν τῷ κόσμῳ ἦν in vs. 10 and εἰς τὰ ἴδια ἦλθεν in vs. 11 correspond to ὃ γέγονεν ἐν αὐτῷ in vs. 4?

Vss. 1:3-4 (*Reading II*)	Vss. 1:10-11
All things came into being through him	The world came into being through him
What appeared in him	He was in the world He came to his own

(v) The incarnational interpretation of John 1:4 (*Reading II*) fits with the incarnational emphasis of the whole Prologue. Here we do not mean only that John 1:4, interpreted in this way, augments by one the references in the Prologue to the incarnation. More important, a loose parallelism may be seen in the incarnational expression in John 1:4,

What has appeared in him was life, and the life was the light of men.

and vs. 9,

The true light, which illuminates every man, was coming into the world.[118]

---

[117] Such similarities, continuities, and cross-referencing in the Prologue are not incompatible with our view of the Prologue as, at least for the most part, an anthology of short Johannine pieces. That the lines of the Prologue should bear throughout the same literary and theological stamp is exactly what would be expected.

[118] Our interpretation of this ambiguous but, for us, important verse is supported by the majority of modern scholars (cf. Brown, *The Gospel according to John*, I, pp. 9f.). That ἐρχόμενον modifies τὸ φῶς rather than ἄνθρωπον is supported by passages elsewhere in John, especially in 3:19 and 12:46, and by the reference which follows immediately to the presence of the Logos in the world (vs. 10); that the imperfect ἦν goes with the participle ἐρχόμενον is supported by John's penchant for the periphrastic construction, often at the beginning of sentences and sometimes with many intervening words, as in 18:18b. But see the contrary observations of Peder Borgen, who nonetheless also thinks that the verse involves the incarnation of the Logos ("Logos was the True Light," pp. 122ff.), and the full study by Benedetto Prete, "La Concordanza del Participio ἐρχόμενον in Giov. 1:9," *Bibbia et Oriente*, 17 (1975), pp. 195ff.

and vs. 14,

> And the Logos became flesh and dwelt with us, full of grace and truth;
> and we beheld his glory. . . .

and vs. 17,[119]

> . . . grace and truth came through Jesus Christ.

All of these involve the same three ideas: (1) the advent (2) of light, glory,
etc. (3) in or through the Logos.

(vi) Finally, the incarnational interpretation of John 1:4 (*Reading II*) is
supported by a comparison with the opening verses of the First Epistle
of John:

> What was from the beginning, what we have heard, what we have
> seen with our eyes, what we have looked at and touched with our hands,
> regarding the word of life—the life was made visible, and we have seen
> and witness and proclaim to you the life eternal which was with God and was
> made visible to us—that which we have seen and have heard we declare also
> to you. . . .[120]

As indicated already in the Introduction, we believe that there is a specific
literary and theological connection between I John 1:1-4 and the Prologue
of the Fourth Gospel, and that I John 1:1-4, itself a Prologue to the First
Epistle, was a kind of model upon which at least some of the material in
the Prologue to the Fourth Gospel was based.[121] Whatever one may think
of this claim, at least the literary and theological relationship between

---

[119] To the observation that vss. 14 and 17 also refer to the incarnation but involve the
aorist rather than the perfect form of γίνομαι, we would respond that the tense in these
verses is not controlled, as is the tense in vs. 4a as well as all the verb tenses in vss. 1-5,
by the progressive salvation-historical sequence of the hymn in vss. 1-5. This response
recalls, of course, our hypothesis about the "mosaic" character of the Prologue, but also
anticipates important points yet to be made in the following chapter.

[120] For a grammatically (though not substantially) quite different way of construing
these lines, see Raymond E. Brown, *The Epistles of John* (Garden City, N.Y.: Doubleday,
1982), p. 151.

[121] So also Robinson, "The Relation of the Prologue to the Gospel of St. John," pp.
123f. Brown, as an example of one who sees the relation very differently, regards the I
John prologue as written in imitation and as a reinterpretation of the Gospel prologue,
against those who, though not full-fledged Docetists, were distorting it in the direction of
Doceticism (*The Epistles of John*, pp. 178, 180ff.). He correctly notes that "it is hardly con-
ceivable that the author who wrote the [Gospel] Prologue with its careful staircase parallelism
. . . and clear line of thought would later write the more awkward I John Prologue" (p.
179), but explains this awkwardness as stemming from "an attempt to give familiar wording a different emphasis" (p. 181). The priority of the I John prologue over the Gospel
prologue seems to me, however, to be simpler and more natural: It best accomodates not
only what we regard as the common authorship of the two documents (*contra* Brown, who
nonetheless provides a judicious and summarizing discussion of this point (pp. 19ff.)), but
especially the apparent development from "the Word of life" (I John 1:1) to the Christological
title "Word" (John 1:1, 14).

these two pieces and their common origin in the Johannine theological circle must be acknowledged. The parallels both in the specific use of language and in the general theme in I John 1:1-4 and John 1:1-18 are unmistakable.[122] Most notably, it can hardly be denied that the incarnation of the Logos is the central and recurring theme in both passages. In I John 1:1-4 expressions which bear on the historical-empirical character of the incarnate Logos tumble out almost on top of one another: He was heard, touched with hands, seen with eyes, made visible, etc. Likewise throughout John 1:1-18: The light was coming into the world, he was in the world, he came to his own, and, of course, the incarnational copestone in vs. 14, ". . . the Logos became flesh and dwelt with us, and we beheld his glory. . . ."

On the basis of the undeniable similarities and parallels between the Prologue to the Epistle and the Prologue to the Gospel it would seem appropriate to ask, specifically, whether in John 1:4a (*Reading II*) we have a concise statement of what is otherwise and more extensively expressed in I John 1:1-2. John 1:4a (1) begins with a neuter relative pronoun with a perfect tense verb (ὃ γέγονεν), (2) involves, on the incarnational interpretation, a reference to the historical advent of the Logos, and (3) immediately links the Logos (or at least what has appeared in him) with life. Alongside this we should note in I John 1:1-2 (1) the frequent use of the neuter relative pronoun with perfect tense verbs (ὃ ἀκηκόαμεν, ὃ ἑωράκαμεν), (2) the pervasive interest in the historical and empirical aspects of the incarnate *logos*, and (3) the direct linking of the *logos* with life. In a word, it is difficult to resist the conclusion that the incarnational language in I John 1:1-2, ". . . what we have seen with our eyes . . . regarding the *logos* of life . . . and the life was made visible, and we have seen ...," is not similarly found in John 1:4a (*Reading II*), "That which has appeared in him [the Logos] was life. . . ." Incidentally, once the incarnational interpretation of John 1:4a has been adopted, then our translation of γέγονεν as "has appeared" (in any event a possible meaning) is surely supported by the references to seeing, eyes, and visibility in I John 1:1-2.

It remains to ask how the incarnational interpretation of John 1:4a fits with the distinction between *Reading II-A* and *Reading II-B*. It will be recalled that the difference is one of punctuation:

Reading II-A: ὃ γέγονεν ἐν αὐτῷ, ζωὴ ἦν. . . .

Reading II-B: ὃ γέγονεν, ἐν αὐτῷ ζωὴ ἦν. . . .

---

[122] Aside from the questions of priority and common authorship, see Brown's list of parallelisms (*The Epistles of John*, p. 179).

It was seen that the metaphysical, existential, naturalistic, and *imago Dei* interpretations all employed *Reading II-B*. This is because they all took ὅ γέγονεν as referring in one way or another to something created, and *Reading II-B*, rather than *II-A*, immediately lends itself to this view. But we have now rejected this view and have argued that ὅ γέγονεν is to be taken not as referring in any way to the created order but rather to the advent of the Logos and life. When this is once granted, then it is as easy to render the line after the manner of *Reading II-A*, "What has appeared in him, was life," as it is to render it in the manner of *Reading II-B*, "What has appeared, in it (*or* him) was life." Inasmuch as both forms of punctuating the line are easily adapted to the incarnational interpretation of John 1:4a, the decision between *Reading II-A* and *II-B* turns out to be a purely stylistic or grammatical one.

Attention has been called repeatedly to the clumsy, anacoluthic character of *Reading II-B*. But we have seen also that, though unnatural, this punctuation is not impossible, and that such expressions occur elsewhere in John. If, on the other side, one decides for *Reading II-A*, then a question arises concerning the meaning of the ἐν. Is it positional (the life which was *in* him appeared) or instrumental (the life has appeared *through* or *by means of* him)? We have already noted that in the numerous instances of ἐν in John's Gospel and Epistles the vast preponderance of them clearly indicate not instrumentality but position. And it is especially difficult not to see a parallel between the ζωὴν ἔχειν ἐν ἑαυτῷ of 5:26, where the ἐν is clearly positional, and the ἐν αὐτῷ ζωὴ ἦν of 1:4a. Still, it somewhat favors the instrumental interpretation of ἐν at 1:4a that the Logos is emphasized throughout John as *being* the life and light, rather than *having* it. All in all, we have a subjective preference for the interpretation of ἐν as positional, but, as a matter of fact, the question poses no problem at all either for *Reading II-A* or the incarnational interpretation thereof. On the other hand, our inclination continues to be to reject *Reading II-B* in favor of *Reading II-A* out of grammatical/stylistic considerations. In any case (and this is the important point here), the decision between *Reading II-A* and *Reading II-B* is not relevant for our general thesis. Both readings can easily bear the incarnational interpretation.

These, then, are the several lines of consideration which may be adduced in support of the incarnational interpretation of John 1:4 (*Reading II*).[123] Some of them are no doubt more relevant and more

---

[123] A sometimes differing expression of some of these points may be found in Lacan, ("L'Oeuvre du Verbe Incarné," pp. 69ff.), Vawter ("What Came To Be in Him was Life (Jn. 1:3b-4a)," pp.403ff.), and Lamarche, ("Le Prologue de Jean," pp. 523ff.). A still further evidence for the incarnational interpretation is advanced by Fredric Schlatter who relates the neuter ὅ with the neuters in Matt. 1:20 and Luke 1:35 ("The Problem of Jn.

forceful than others, but all of them converge on the same point and together they constitute impressive evidence. Then, too, it must be remembered that attempts to make a different sense of the passage have not been successful. Unless therefore we revert, *haud credibile*, to *Reading I*, and if we insist on a clear and decisive meaning for *Reading II*, the incarnational interpretation emerges as the most plausible.

And we maintain this view against Brown who mentions in passing those few who have seen in vs. 4 a reference to the incarnation and then passes off this whole approach with a two-part objection. We take the second of these first:

> . . . the editor of the Prologue has inserted a reference to John the Baptist *after* vs. 5, and one can scarcely imagine that the editor would introduce John the Baptist after describing the ministry of Jesus and its effect. Clearly the editor thought that the references to the coming of Jesus began in vs. 10; he put the coming of John the Baptist in vss. 6-8 before the coming of Jesus, and used vs. 9 to connect John the Baptist to the moment of that coming. Of course, the editor could have misunderstood the import of vss. 4-5, but he was much closer to the original hymn than we are.[124]

In addition to begging the question ("Clearly the editor thought that the references to the coming of Jesus began in vs. 10"), Brown appears to know a great deal about the redaction of the Prologue. On the basis of the evidence in the Prologue we suspect, in fact, that there was no redaction of the Prologue of the sort Brown envisions. In the Introduction we portrayed the Prologue as a kind of mosaic or anthology of Johannine pieces including a complete Logos hymn, some miscellaneous poetic or hymnic lines, some narrative material, and some later interpolations, and we spoke of a grafting of this loosely connected material onto the original beginning of the Gospel; we even suggested (with the support of several other exegetes) that the narrative material in vss. 6-8 was the original beginning of the Gospel. If anything like this was at all the case then Brown is obviously attempting to understand the internal relations of the Prologue from a false perspective.

Brown's first objection to the incarnational interpretation of John 1:4 is more interesting. He says,

> . . . a jump from creation in vs. 3 to the coming of Jesus in 4 seems exceedingly abrupt, especially when the "that which had come to be" in 4

1:3b-4a," pp. 56ff.), but the argument seems to me to be strained and otherwise problematic.

[124] Brown, *The Gospel according to John*, I, p. 26.

is a link to "came to be" in 3. If vss. 4-5 refer to the coming of Jesus, then the clearer reference to his coming in 9 and 10 seems tautological.[125]

To begin with, the points made in our paragraph above (the Prologue contains independent and disparate material, etc.) would seem relevant also to Brown's concern about the tautology, but in any case the point of vs. 10 is not the Logos' presence in the world but the rejection of the incarnate Logos by the world he created, thus there is in vss. 4 and 10 no real tautology. Further, and aside from the question as to what sort of "link" is involved between vss. 4a and 3b, we do not find the jump from creation in vs. 3 to the incarnation of the Logos in vs. 4 to be "exceedingly abrupt," at least no more so than the jump from the Logos' pre-existent relation to God in vss. 1-2 to his creative relation to the world in vs. 3. In fact, as will be evident in our last chapter, we find in the hymnic lines of John 1:1-5 four "moments," and consequently "jumps," in the progressive saving activity of the Logos, and that these moments constitute the logic and theology of a complete Logos hymn.

---

[125] Brown, *The Gospel according to John*, I, p. 26. Note also the similar complaint of Feuillet: ". . . on a de la peine à croire que déjà la pensée de l'auteur aille exclusivement au Christ présent parmi les hommes, alors que le mystère de l'Incarnation ne sera mentionné formellement qu'au v. 14" (*Le Prologue du Quatrième Évangile*, p. 40).

CHAPTER THREE

THE THEOLOGY

The hymnic lines in John 1:1-5, as with much else in the Fourth Gospel, were composed with great care. On this there is universal agreement. But the logical and theological structure of this passage—the order, progression, and completeness of ideas there—is no doubt even richer than has usually been supposed. As it turns out, the key to the meaning of John 1:1-5 is the incarnational interpretation of vs. 4a. Thus only now are we in a position to develop the interpretation of the whole passage. Recalling the twofold thesis of the present work, our interpretation will illuminate John 1:1-5 as regards first its theological structure, which, we will argue, turns out to be a salvation-historical one, and also its literary structure, which, we believe, turns out to embrace an entire Christological hymn.

The Logic of the Logos Hymn

As with the Prologue as a whole, scholars have organized and interpreted the material even in John 1:1-5 in widely different and often irreconcilable ways. We do not intend here to consider individually the various proposals concerning the organization and meaning of this passage. We proceed, rather, somewhat like Copernicus, pleading for a different standpoint from which the data are found to yield immediately a simpler and more elegant interpretation.[1] In this instance, the datum is John 1:1-5, the new standpoint is the incarnational interpretation of 1:4a, and the new interpretation is a salvation-historical one.

We begin by recalling some points from the Introduction. From a purely literary and aesthetic standpoint alone we are persuaded that John 1:1-5 involves a Christological hymn. The hymnic character of the passage is suggested by the exalted language, the Christological concentration employing the metaphor/title Logos, the four *parallelismi membrorum*, the staircase parallelisms which appear to be a structuring principle more or less throughout, the relative length of the lines, and the way in which the ideas in the lines suggest couplets in vss. 1a-b, 3-5. We argued further for the deletion of vss. 1c and 2 from the original hymnic material on the grounds that these lines, unlike the other lines in John 1:1-5, form no

---

[1] Of course, this procedure will be resisted by those scholars who appear to place a high value on *enodatio involutior!*

parallelism and otherwise bear every mark of being later polemical intrusions. Of course this latter must remain uncertain and in any event is not crucial for our general thesis. Nonetheless, if it is accepted, then on *Reading II* of John 1:3-4 we are left with the following four strophes:

I. ἐν ἀρχῇ ἦν ὁ λόγος,
   καὶ ὁ λόγος ἦν πρὸς τὸν θεόν.

II. πάντα δι' αὐτοῦ ἐγένετο,
    καὶ χωρὶς αὐτοῦ ἐγένετο οὐδὲ ἕν.

III. ὃ γέγονεν ἐν αὐτῷ ζωὴ ἦν,
     καὶ ἡ ζωὴ ἦν τὸ φῶς τῶν ἀνθρώπων.

IV. καὶ τὸ φῶς ἐν τῇ σκοτίᾳ φαίνει,
    καὶ ἡ σκοτία αὐτὸ οὐ κατέλαβεν.

These we propose as the hymnic lines in John 1:1-5 from a purely literary standpoint. From a *logical* standpoint there is more to be said, and here our incarnational interpretation of vs. 4a is critical. We note that each strophe is a logical unit in itself, each declaring its own distinctive idea. More specifically, and on our incarnational interpretation of vs. 4a, each strophe makes an assertion about the Logos' relation to something, and, in each strophe, to something different. Thus, the theme of Strophe I is the Logos in his personal relation to God; Strophe II expresses the Logos' creative relation to the world; Strophe III expresses the Logos in his incarnate and salvific relation to men; and Strophe IV turns our attention to the Logos' victorious relation to evil.[2]

The theme of Strophe I is hardly mistakable. Both λόγος and θεός are explicitly mentioned, and the nature of the Logos' relationship to God is suggested by the preposition πρός which emphasizes a sort of communion between the two persons. With respect to Strophe II, we have argued in an earlier context (against Pollard's "wider" interpretation, and in agreement with almost all commentators) that πάντα refers to the world, and that the whole verse asserts the Logos' creative relation to the world. Especially relevant here is vs. 10b which we take to be a parallel statement which substitutes κόσμος for πάντα; also relevant is the way in which the first words of the Prologue, ἐν ἀρχῇ, are identical to the first words of the Septuagint and thus are surely intended as a deliberate echo of Gen. 1:1.

---

[2] Cf. Lacan's strikingly similar but *three*-stage logical organization of vss. 1-5 ("L'Oeuvre du Verbe Incarné," p. 72). My own four-stage organization was conceived independently of Lacan's work and, as we will see, better accommodates the full content and language of the passage.

The interpretation of Strophe III would be fraught with difficulties except for the fact that we have just invested nearly a hundred pages in this question. The reference to men, ἀνθρώπων, is at least explicit; we have shown earlier that ζωή here and everywhere in John means spiritual life and thus, again, men, the subject of such life, are involved; and in the case of the pronoun in the phrase ἐν αὐτῷ, we have opted for a masculine ("in him") rather than a neuter ("in it"), requiring λόγος as the antecedent. Strophe IV is not as difficult as some commentators think. Already in vs. 4 light has been equated with the spiritual life that is, or at least is in, the Logos. This, plus other Johannine (spiritual) light-references (most notably John 8:12), leaves no doubt that the Logos, or at least the Logos' light, is the subject of vs. 5a. This in turn dictates a symbolic meaning for "darkness" in vs. 5b, and its meaning here is in any event determined by its symbolic usage elsewhere in John (e.g. John 8:12, 12:35, 46; I John 1:5; 2:8) and the light/darkness dualism that characterizes his writings. Thus σκοτία here signifies, as most commentators agree, the whole realm of evil.

But this fourfold division of the hymn not only represents the Logos as standing in four relations (to God, the world, man, and evil), but also as standing in these relations in four moments or stages or periods which succeed one another in time. Strophe I refers to the Logos in his pre-existent state; Strophe II moves forward to a statement about the Logos at the time of creation; Strophe III moves the thought forward to the time of the Logos' incarnation; and Strophe IV expresses the Logos' activity in the present (from the writer's standpoint). Further, we think it hardly an accident that four different verb tenses are associated with the four units, each unit being dominated by a different tense. This is obviously true of the first two units. The imperfect ἦν occurs exclusively in the first, and the aorist ἐγένετο occurs exclusively in the second. It is not so obvious in the third unit where we encounter the perfect γέγονεν, an imperfect ἦν (or, unlikely, a present ἐστίν-become-ἦν), and another ἦν; nor is it so clear in the fourth unit where we have a present φαίνει and an aorist κατέλαβεν. Notwithstanding the facts that the perfect tense is not carried through consistently in the third section, and the present tense is not carried through consistently in the fourth, we believe that the perfect and the present signal the temporal aspect of, respectively, the third and fourth units just as the imperfect does in the first unit and the aorist does in the second.

With respect to the third unit, we emphasize first the introduction of the perfect γέγονεν over against the preceding imperfects (ἦν) of vs. 1 and aorists (ἐγένετο) of vs. 3. R.H. Lightfoot is clearly wrong when he says that "in 1:5a the past tense, used throughout 1:1-4, is dropped in favor of the present tense," this to remind the reader that the light evident in creation and explaining man's true nature continues even yet to shine.[3] Aside from our rejection of Lightfoot's identification of ὃ γέγονεν with creation, how can it be said that the past tense is "used throughout 1:1-4"? The verb γέγονεν is most certainly not a simple past tense; it has already been stressed that the Greek perfect (difficult to render into English) is more of a present than a past tense inasmuch as it emphasizes the continuing present results of a past occurrence.[4] Aland too sees vs. 1-4 as a single unit, asserting that the text "in vv. 1-4 nur mit ἦν operiert und erst mit vs. 5 in Präsens übergeht."[5] It is, says Aland, this prevailing employment of the imperfect ἦν that unites vss. 1-4 into a unit. According to Aland, vss. 1-4 deal with pre-fallen creation, whereas vs. 5, with its present φαίνει, deals in one sentence with the state of creation after the Fall.[6] But it is, of course, arguable whether ἦν is the operative verb in vss. 1-4, and Aland's explanation of ὃ γέγονεν will surely strike many as forced: "Das Perfekt ὃ γέγονεν versteht sich aus der Fortdauer der Schöpfung von einst. . . ."[7] This is not to mention, again, that such an interpretation of ὃ γέγονεν must reckon with our earlier rejection of ὃ γέγονεν as referring in any way to creation.

Against Lightfoot, Aland, and any others who say that the scene changes from the past to the present only with vs. 4, we must raise, further, an old point. It will be recalled that in various MSS. the first ἦν, and sometimes both occurrences, of vs. 4 are given as the present ἐστίν, presumably (on *Reading II*) to bring the two verbs into accord with the perceived temporal force of the perfect γέγονεν. Although these readings must be rejected, they show nonetheless that in antiquity the starkness of the perfect γέγονεν, in contrast to the imperfects and aorists going before, was not unappreciated as it is by some today. It was, however, appreciated by Zahn, who, though taking a very different view of this whole question, observed,

> Das Perf. γέγονεν, welches nach dem zweimaligen ἐγένετο um so mehr ins Ohr fällt, versetz den Leser in die Gegenwart und bezeichnet das in der Gegenwart Existirende als das fertige Produkt des vollendeten Werdens.[8]

Howard's statement that

---

[3] R. H. Lightfoot, *St. John's Gospel: A Commentary with the Revised Version Text*, ed. C. F. Evans (Oxford, England: Oxford University Press, 1956), p. 79.

[4] See above, p. 81, note 13.

[5] Aland, "Eine Untersuchung zu Joh. 1:3-4," p. 206.

[6] Aland, "Eine Untersuchung zu Joh. 1:3-4," p. 207.

[7] Aland, "Eine Untersuchung zu Joh. 1:3-4," p. 207.

[8] Zahn, *Das Evangelium des Johannes*, p. 52.

the contrast is between the perfect tense (γέγονεν) and the imperfect (ἦν),
between that which has been created in time and still exists, and that which
was before time began. . . .[9]

does some justice to the perfect γέγονεν and is surely an improvement on
Lightfoot and Aland, but it is still inadequate. It yet confuses into two
what is actually a three-fold distinction. The contrast is, rather, between
the imperfect (ἦν), the aorist (ἐγένετο), and the perfect (γέγονεν); between
that which was before creation, that which happened once upon a time,
and that which has happened and continues even yet. It remains, finally,
to emphasize that this unit *begins* with the perfect tense, immediately
throwing the unit into contrast with the preceding ones and introducing
a new temporal moment.

With respect to the fourth unit, it is obvious that our interpretation
resists any view of κατέλαβεν as representing a simple past event, though
this latter would not, of course, be utterly incompatible with our proposed
scheme. On the other hand, it is possible to take it as a gnomic aorist
expressing "an act which is valid for all time,"[10] in which case the line
would mean that the darkness did not overcome it and never will, and,
with some justification, could be rendered as "the darkness cannot put
it out." Or it could be argued that οὐ κατέλαβεν refers at least to the same
time-frame as the somewhat parallel οὐκ ἔγνω of vs. 10 and οὐ παρέλαβον
of vs. 11, namely, the earthly appearance of the Logos and thus the (for
the author) recent past.[11] In either case, the interpretation fits the present
tense φαίνει, and it agrees too with the imagery involved in the strikingly
similar Johannine statement, ". . . the darkness is passing away and the
true light is already shining" (I John 2:8). It is also important to note
that, again, this unit *begins* with the present tense.

To be sure, if the perfect tense were employed exclusively in the third
unit, and the present tense in the fourth unit, our thesis about the four-
fold division of John 1:1-5 would be more certain—perhaps irresistible.
Nevertheless, it is a fact that each of the four units is introduced with a
different tense, and it is our intuition that these initial tenses establish the
temporal aspect of units III and IV, no less than I and II. It is more than
an intuition that when these four temporal aspects are considered
together they yield a temporal succession represented as four periods, or

---

[9] W. F. Howard (with A. J. Gossip), *The Gospel according to St. John*, in the *Interpreter's
Bible*, VIII (New York: Abindgon, 1952), p. 465.

[10] Blass/Debrunner, *A Greek Grammar of the New Testament and Other Early Christian
Literature*, sect. 333 (but cf. Zerwick's warning about artificial appeals to the gnomic aorist
to solve difficulties (*Biblical Greek*, sect. 256)). Or we may have here a "complexive" aorist,
signifying a summation or terminus of repeated (here *attempted*) actions (sect. 332).

[11] Thus, for example, Siegfried Schulz, *Das Evangelium nach Johannes* (Göttingen:
Vandenhoeck & Ruprecht, 1972), pp. 20f.

perhaps better, moments, stretching from the Logos' pre-existence to the present.[12] From start to finish, these lines are controlled by the ideas of temporality and history. (And the first lines are no exception. Some, such as Bernard, suggest that the imperfect ἦν in the first two lines "is expressive . . . of continuous timeless existence."[13] But aside from the question of what a *continuous* timeless existence could possibly be, it is very doubtful that the New Testament authors entertained any idea of such an existence. I would say, in fact, that the present passage is just more evidence that their perspectives were thoroughly conditioned by the categories of time and history.)

Yet another refinement of these lines is possible. For it may be argued further (from a literary and stylistic standpoint) that the incarnational reference in vs. 4 is central to the hymn. First, we may appeal to the somewhat aesthetic and subjective impression that the two strophes preceding and the one following provide a sort of dramatic heightening of Strophe III. More concretely, the centrality of the incarnational reference in the first line of Strophe III is suggested by the way in which it divides and structures the hymn into two parts concerning the pre-incarnate and post-incarnate Logos. Strophe I is structured by a staircase progression (A→B, B→C), whereas Strophe II is not; but Strophes III and IV are structured by one continuous staircase progression (A→B, B→C, C→D, D→E). This suggests, however mildly, that Strophes III and IV were conceived together in some degree of contrast with the earlier strophes, the contrast being established by the incarnational reference. These latter observations are offered only as tentative suggestions. But if they are accepted then the high point of the hymn is the affirmation of the incarnation, and this in any event is just what one would expect of a Johannine hymn.

All of this may now be summarized. Strophe I represents the Logos in his pre-existent and personal communion with God before creation. Strophe II moves us forward in time to the moment of creation and represents the Logos in his creating relationship to the world. Strophe III moves us forward to the decisive event of the incarnation of the Logos whom it represents as having stood historically in a salvation-imparting relation to men. Strophe IV leaves behind the past stages of the Logos'

---

[12] These four moments might profitably be compared with the three stages of the hymn in Phil. 2:6-11: pre-existence, earthly ministry, exaltation. On the three stages, see R. P. Martin, *Carmen Christi: Philippians ii. 5-11 in Recent Interpretation and in the Setting of Early Christian Worship* (Cambridge, England: Cambridge University Press, 1967), pp. 22f. and the literature cited in n. 3. On the three Christological moments as characteristic of all primitive Christological hymns see S. de Ausejo, "¿Es un Himno a Cristo el Pròlogo de San Juan?," *passim*.

[13] Bernard, *A Critical and Exegetical Commentary on the Gospel according to St. John*, p. 2.

redemptive activity and extols the Logos in his present and continuing victory over evil. This logical and theological organization of the lines in John 1:1-5 reinforces the conviction that we have here a Christological hymn in four strophes. More specifically this logical and theological interpretation of the lines provides a complete meaning for the four strophes—a complete picture, a complete dramatic representation, a beginning, a middle, and an end—and this suggests that the strophes before us constitute the whole of a Christological hymn. Still more on the theological side, the representation here of the four successive moments of the Logos' redemptive history clearly discloses the salvation-historical perspective that constitutes this Christological hymn. It is a hymn in which the early Johannine community celebrated the salvation-history enacted through the Logos:

    I. In the beginning was the Logos,
       And the Logos was with God.

   II. All things came into being through him,
       And apart from him nothing came into being.

  III. What appeared in him was Life,
       And the Life was the Light of men.

   IV. And the Light shines in the Darkness,
       And the Darkness cannot overcome it.

It is sometimes observed, correctly, that in ancient Jewish literature the border between poetry and prose was not nearly so fixed as it is in modern literature. Nonetheless, the hymnodic starkness of the above lines, from both a literary and theological standpoint, throws them into immediate contrast with anything else—however poetic—in the remainder of the Fourth Gospel. We venture, moreover, that this Logos hymn was a liturgical[14] and even antiphonal piece.[15] The structure of four two-line couplets, each advancing on the thought of the previous ones, lends itself perfectly to antiphonal recitation. One can easily imagine the precentor intoning the first line of each couplet and the congregation responding in unison with the second, throughout the four salvation-historical stanzas.[16] That hymns were employed by the earliest Christians

---

[14] Jeremias states outrightly (on what grounds I do not know) that the Logos hymn of the (hypothesized) *Urprolog* "was one of the hymns sung at the daily Eucharist" ("The Revealing Word," pp. 74f.).

[15] See Martin's succinct discussion of early Christian hymnody and antiphonal recitation (and the literature cited) in *Carmen Christi*, pp. 1ff.

[16] So Jeremias: "The Prologue is constructed by means of parallelism, the pairing of similarly sounding clauses, constituting a kind of call and response—perhaps echoing the alternation between precentor and congregation" ("The Revealing Word," p. 72).

we know, of course, from the New Testament itself (for instance, Eph. 5:19, Col. 3:16, Jas. 5:13). We know too that antiphonal recitation was a practice of Jewish origin and that Christian antiphonal hymnody existed at least as early as (and, under the influence of Jewish practice, perhaps much earlier than?) Pliny's report, when he was governor of Pontus and Bithynia in Asia Minor in 111-12 A. D., about the Christians there who regularly came together "carmenque Christo quasi deo secum *invicem.*"[17] The Logos hymn of John 1:1a-b, 3-5 might easily have been one such hymn.

Salvation-History and the Fourth Gospel

It is nothing new to view the lines in John 1:1-5 as containing hymnic material and as being at least part of a Christological hymn. It *is* new, however, to argue as we have that John 1:1-5 involves the whole of a Christological hymn and that it is, more specifically, a salvation-history hymn. On the other hand, it is important to recall that our primary thesis is that, independently of the question of a hymn, these lines involve, at least, a salvation-historical perspective.

The idea of salvation-history, *Heilsgeschichte*, cannot simply be waved about as a *Zauberbegriff* which causes everything to fall in place and solves all problems. Indeed, it itself is not unproblematic. Over the last hundred years or so the expression "salvation-history" has been employed by a long line of thinkers and with often differing emphases.[18] But it was catapulted to the center of theological discussion most notably through the contributions of Oscar Cullmann, and of course there was catapulted with it the peculiarly Cullmannian *Heilsgeschichte* emphasis. In saying that the Logos Hymn in John 1:1-5 is a *salvation-history* hymn, we intend something consonant with Cullmann's use of the expression. This encompasses both a wider and narrower emphasis. The *wider* emphasis stresses, at a minimum, that history is revelatory and redemptive, and, specifically, that God has acted for man's salvation in the starkly historical-empirical ministry, death, and resurrection of Jesus Christ. The *narrower*, and more peculiarly Cullmannian, emphasis entails the further idea of a temporal succession of divine, salvific acts bound to one another by the elements of continuity and progression.[19]

---

[17] See Martin's discussions of the significance of Pliny's report and specifically the meaning of *carmen* and *secum invicem* (and the literature cited) in *Carmen Christi*, pp. 1ff.

[18] Before his untimely death, Leonhard Goppelt provided a brief representation of many *heilsgeschichtliche* thinkers in his *Theologie des Neuen Testaments*, I, ed. Jurgen Roloff (Göttingen: Vandenhoeck & Ruprecht, 1975), pp. 45ff.

[19] Cullmann's salvation-historical perspective tends to pervade all of his writings but is developed most explicitly in *Christus und die Zeit: Die urchristliche Zeit- und Geschichtsauf-*

Setting aside, for the moment, all criteria except one, it may reasonably be insisted that while any Christian theology rightfully rests with a kind of sense for the configuration of the Biblical witness as a whole, it must in the end justify itself on the basis of concrete texts, and, whenever possible, those texts which give self-conscious expression to that theological perspective. We believe that the theology of salvation-history, certainly in the wide sense and to some degree also in the narrow sense, is justified not only from the Biblical witness as a whole but also on the basis of self-consciously salvation-historical texts. As regards the New Testament, most scholars, and even those who are critical of the theology of salvation-

---

fassung (Zollikon-Zurich: Evangelischer Verlag, 1946), the later (and already cited) *Heil als Geschichte*, and, in a way, in *Die Christologie des Neuen Testaments*, 4th ed. (Tübingen: Mohr, 1966) of which the idea of salvation-history is the organizing principle. In addition to the ideas of succession, continuity, and progression, the central thesis that *"alle christliche Theologie ihrem innersten Wesen nach biblische Geschichte ist"* (*Christus und die Zeit*, p. 19) is unfolded in terms of an already/not-yet eschatology, the principle of representation, and a functional Christology. It is ironic that one of the best summaries of Cullmann's position is provided by Rudolf Bultmann as a preface to his trenchant critique in 1948 of *Christus und die Zeit*, "Heilsgeschichte und Geschichte: Zu O. Cullmann, Christus und die Zeit," *TL*, 73 (1948), pp. 659ff. This remains an excellent summary even after the publication of *Heil als Geschichte*, though Cullmann does introduce there new ideas. For a recent and extended representation of Cullmann's position as a whole, see Hans-Georg Hermesmann, *Zeit und Heil: Oscar Cullmanns Theologie der Heilsgeschichte* (Paderborn: Bonifacius, 1979). One might mention also: Jean Frisque, *Oscar Cullmann: Une Théologie de l'Histoire du Salut* (Tournai: Casterman, 1960); Karlfried Fröhlich, "Die Mitte des Neuen Testaments: Oscar Cullmanns Beiträge zur Theologie der Gegenwart," in *Oikonomia: Heilsgeschichte als Thema der Theologie*, ed. Felix Christ (Hamburg: Reich, 1967), pp. 203ff. Not surprisingly Cullmann has been attacked from many sides. Cullmann answered his critics in an introductory chapter to the third edition of *Christus und die Zeit*, and further refined and restated his position, *vis à vis* his opponents, in *Heil als Geschichte*, most notably Bultmann, "Heilsgeschichte und Geschichte," pp. 659ff., Buri, "Das Problem der ausgebliebenen Parusie," *STU*, 16 (1946), pp. 97ff., and Karl Gerhard Steck, *Die Idee der Heilsgeschichte: Hofmann-Schlatter-Cullmann* (Zollikon-Zurich: Evangelischer Verlag, 1959), pp. 43ff. (Buri was specifically answered in the earlier "Zur Diskussion des Problems der ausgebliebenen Parusie: Replik," *TZ*, 3 (1947), pp. 422ff.). Still more recent critiques include the not-so-well conceived treatment by Geiko Müller-Fahrenholz, *Heilsgeschichte zwischen Ideologie und Prophetie: Profile und Kritik heilsgeschichtlicher Theorien der ökumenischen Bewegung zwischen 1948 und 1968* (Freiburg/Breisgau: Herder, 1974), pp. 137ff., and the more sympathetic discussion by Wolfhart Pannenberg in his essay "Weltgeschichte und Heilsgeschichte," in *Geschichte-Ereignis und Erzählung*, ed. Reinhart Koselleck and Wolf-Dieter Stempel (Munich: Wilhelm Fink, 1973), pp. 315ff. For a summary of Cullmann's interaction with his critics, see Hermesmann, *Zeit und Heil*, Sect. G. A sampling of other relevant literature: K. Löwith, *Meaning in History: The Theological Implications of the Philosophy of History* (Chicago: University of Chicago Press, 1949), Ch. 11; Franz Hesse, *Abschied von der Heilsgeschichte* (Zurich: Theologischer Verlag, 1971); Günter Klein, "Bibel und Heilsgeschichte," *ZNW*, 62 (1971), pp. 1ff.; W. G. Kümmel, "Heilsgeschichte im Neuen Testament?" in *Neues Testament und Kirche*, ed. J. Gnilka (Freiburg/Breisgau: Herder, 1974), pp. 434ff. A most interesting phenomenon of recent New Testament scholarship is the conversion of Ernst Käsemann, formerly one of Cullmann's fiercest opponents, to a salvation-historical perspective, as in his essay "Rechtfertigung und Heilsgeschichte im Römerbrief," in *Paulinische Perspektiven* (Tübingen: Mohr, 1969), pp. 108ff.

history, concede that the salvation-historical perspective plays an important role in the thought of Paul, and that it controls the entire perspective
of the Lukan Gospel and Acts, especially Stephen's speech in Acts 7 which
is one of the most striking expressions of salvation-history in the entire
Bible. Cullmann, of course, claims to find salvation-history almost everywhere, including what many would regard as the most unlikely of places:
the Fourth Gospel.

With Cullmann we reject Bultmann's influential view of the Fourth
Gospel according to which demythologization has been carried out in this
document, the original futuristic elements in Jesus' proclamation having
been radically reinterpreted into what we might call "the existential present" with its "call to decision."[20] Cullmann observes that such an interpretation certainly runs in a direction opposite to salvation-history,[21] for
the latter involves, as we have seen, a conception of salvation which
embraces the past, present, and future of a historical movement. Setting
aside other problems with Bultmann's view of the Fourth Gospel,[22] his
particular existential interpretation[23] of this Gospel also runs in a direction opposite to the Fourth Gospel itself if Cullmann is right (as I believe
he is) in finding salvation-history here too. In fact, "Heilsgeschichte im
Johannesevangelium [ist] nicht nur *auch* vorhanden, sondern sogar in
betonter Weise,"[24] and "decision" in the Fourth Gospel, for all of its
importance, presupposes and is founded on this salvation-historical
perspective:

> Anstatt [Bultmanns] "immer in der Entscheidung stehen" würde ich, wie
> überall im Neuen Testament, so ganz besonders hier sagen: "in der Ent-
> scheidung stehen auf Grund des Hineingestelltseins in einen göttlichen
> Heilsplan, der die Zeit und die Welten umfasst."[25]

Cullmann summarizes his opposition to Bultmann in regard to the interpretation of the Fourth Gospel:

---

[20] Cf. especially Bultmann's commentary, *Das Evangelium des Johannes, passim.*
[21] Cullmann, *Heil als Geschichte,* p. 245.
[22] To say nothing of Bultmann's problematic attempt to derive the Fourth Gospel from
an original Gnostic source, or his strained speculations about the Mandaean milieu of the
original Gospel, his attempt to refer the futuristic passages in John to a later redactor
(who sought to bring the "realized" and "existential" eschatology into harmony with the
more standard view) has been steadily eroded.
[23] The word "particular" ought to be stressed inasmuch as the existential perspective
assumes varying forms and emphases, not all of which are inimical to the salvation-
historical perspective. Aside from the full title, *Heil als Geschichte: Heilsgeschichtliche Existenz
im Neuen Testament,* Cullmann himself relates the salvation-historical perspective to one
kind of existential emphasis.
[24] Cullmann, *Heil als Geschichte,* p. 247.
[25] Cullmann, *Heil als Geschichte,* p. 247.

> Wie Bultmann seine Sicht des ganzen Neuen Testaments durch das Johannesevangelium gerechtfertigt findet, so ich diejenige, die ich in diesem Buch vortrage.[26]

Again:

> Some have falsely used John's Gospel to support the elimination of salvation history. On the contrary, the Gospel of John is a life of Jesus seen entirely from the perspective of salvation history.[27]

The case is made in *Heil als Geschichte*, in a section called "Johannesevangelium und Heilsgeschichte,"[28] and consists of four points:[29] First, John's representation of the historical life of Jesus as the center of God's saving and revelatory activity; second, his emphasis on the relationship between the life of Jesus and the present period of the Church; third, his emphasis on the relationship between the life of Jesus to the past episodes of God's saving actions, even to creation; fourth, his emphasis on the relationship between the life of Jesus to the yet future consummation of the saving process.

We believe that these emphases are, indeed, found in the Fourth Gospel and that the Fourth Gospel does express, though not systematically, a salvation-historical perspective in this narrower as well as the wider sense. Certainly, such a perspective coheres with this Evangelist's pervasive interest in history. Two observations here. First, there has occurred a turning of the tide with respect to the historical value of John, beyond the knowledge it yields about the Johannine community. Admittedly, the Fourth Gospel's interest in the history and facts concerning the life and teaching of Jesus is controlled by the author's theological purpose, but it is no longer possible to regard the Fourth Gospel, by comparison with the Synoptic Gospels, as a sort of symbolic, or mystical, or Gnostic representation of Christ with little relevance for actual history. As regards the quest for the historical Jesus, the relation of the Synoptic accounts of Jesus to that of the Johannine account is still far from clear. On the other hand, it is increasingly recognized on literary-critical grounds that much of the Johannine account is rooted in historical data and may even provide at certain points a more accurate picture than is contained in the Synoptics,[30] and the growing acceptance of a radically early dating of

[26] Cullmann, *Heil als Geschichte*, p. 247.

[27] Oscar Cullmann, "Foundations: The Theology of Salvation History and the Ecumenical Dialogue," in *Vatican II: The New Direction*, ed. James D. Hester, tr. James D. Hester, *et al.* (New York: Harper & Row, 1968), p. 33.

[28] Cullmann, *Heil als Geschichte*, p. 245ff.

[29] Cullmann's discussion here is based on an earlier article "L'Évangile Johannique et l'Histoire du Salut," *NTS*, 11 (1964-65), pp. 111ff.

[30] Cf. C. H. Dodd, *Historical Tradition in the Fourth Gospel* (Cambridge, England: Cambridge University Press, 1965), and the abbreviated discussions in Cullmann, *Der johan-*

John (which I have accepted since 1970[31]) is bound to hold yet further and possibly more general implications for its historical value. Second, and more important, the salvation-historical perspective coheres with John's overarching interest in history as a theological category, as we may call it. Nowhere else in the New Testament is the empirical-historical reality of the incarnate God as living, dying, and raised, and as the fulfillment of the past and promise of the future, so dramatically portrayed. To be sure, there is something to Clement's impression that John's is a "spiritual" Gospel,[32] and we even agree, in a way, with Käsemann's impression that the bulk of John's portrayal of Jesus sounds a decidedly Docetic tone.[33] But this same Evangelist appears to us to have sought to correct this impression—to which he himself may have unwittingly contributed—with the clearly anti-Docetic warnings in I John 4:1-3 (note also II John 8) and the vividly empirical outbursts in I John 1:1-3 and then, not so obviously, in the Prologue material, most notably at 1:14: "And the Logos became flesh, and dwelt with us, and we beheld his glory. . . ."[34]

Here we have only suggested that the relevance of the Fourth Gospel for the history of Jesus and its emphasis on this history as the foundation of the Good News makes this Gospel not an unlikely place, after all, for the discovery of a somewhat more articulated conception of the saving events centered in Jesus Christ, that is, a salvation-historical perspective in the narrower sense. Nonetheless, we believe that Cullmann, as well as any others who have sought to document the salvation-historical perspec-

---

neische Kreis: Sein Platz im Spätjudentum, in der Jüngerschaft Jesu und im Urchristentum (Tübingen: Mohr, 1975), Ch. 3, and Stephen S. Smalley, *John: Evangelist and Interpreter* (Exeter: Paternoster, 1978), pp. 162ff., but especially in John A. T. Robinson, *The Priority of John*, ed. J. F. Coakley (London: S. C. M. Press, 1985).

[31] When F. Lamar Cribbs published his article, "A Reassessment of the Date of Origin and Destination of the Gospel of John," *JBL*, 89 (1970), pp. 38ff. Cf. J. A. T. Robinson, *Redating the New Testament* (Philadelphia: Westminster Press, 1976), ch. 9, and Cullmann: ". . . ich [bin] jetzt im Gegensatz zu früher eher geneigt, die ursprüngliche Abfassung des Evangeliums als zumindest ebenso alt, wahrscheinlich sogar als älter als die des ältesten der synoptischen Evangelien anzusehen." (*Der johanneische Kreis*, p. 101). More recently: Robinson, *The Priority of John*, pp. 67ff., and Friedmar Kemper, "Zur literarischen Gestalt des Johannesevangelium," *TZ*, 43 (1987), pp. 42ff.

[32] Clement of Alexandria as quoted in Eusebius, *Historia Ecclesiastica*, VI, 14, 6 (*PG*, 20, 552f.).

[33] Ernst Käsemann, *Jesu letzter Wille nach Johannes 17* (Tübingen: Mohr, 1966).

[34] We leave aside the question as to the precise nature of the Docetic doctrine advanced by the defectors addressed in I and II John. Suffice it to say that it was at least an incipient Docetism (cf. Brown, *The Epistles of John*, pp. 47ff.). Brown denies utterly any anti-Docetic motivation behind the lines of the Prologue (*The Epistles of John*, pp. 178, 180ff.). Aside from 1:14, we do not insist on the anti-Docetic nature of the Prologue, and even grant that the Prologue itself, with its emphasis on the pre-existence and exaltation of the Logos, could in principle have been appropriated by the (Docetically inclined) adversaries addressed in I John (cf. Brown, *The Epistles of John*, p. 180.).

tive in the Fourth Gospel, have missed the most striking evidence of all. The reason why they have missed it is that there has not been a suitably serious exegesis of John 1:4a (*Reading II*) and consideration of its implications for the whole of John 1:1-5. To be sure, references to the Prologue are scattered throughout Cullmann's works, and in *Christus und die Zeit* he even declared,

> Nirgends hat die Einheitlichkeit allen Offenbarungsgeschehens als eines Christusgeschehens, die im Neuen Testament überall mehr oder weniger vorausgesetzt ist, kraftvolleren Ausdruck gefunden als im Prolog des Johannesevangeliums, wo Schöpfung und Erlösung als ein einziges Christus- und Offenbarungsgeschehen erscheinen.[35]

But the expression of this "Einheitlichkeit allen Offenbarungsgeschehens als eines Christusgeschehens" is, as we have seen, much more powerful than even Cullmann and any others have suspected.

Like a Copernican revolution in the understanding of John 1:1-5, the shift to the incarnational interpretation of vs. 1:4a (*Reading II*) yielded for us a salvation-historical perspective in the whole of the passage. And here we intend not only a salvation-historical perspective in the wide sense (though with the reference to the historical advent of the Logos is vs. 4a that is certainly involved) but also in the narrow sense. Of course not all the features of, say, the Cullmannian idea of salvation-history are present here, but certainly the essential ones are. First, the logical and theological center of these verses (as with the Prologue as a whole and with the Fourth Gospel as a whole) is the historical advent of the Logos (vs. 4a). Second, the advent of the Logos is not presented in isolation but in relationship to and in *continuity* with other stages of God's saving activity, namely, the Logos in his pre-existent relation to God (vs. 1), his creative relation to the world (vs. 3), and his enduring victory over evil (vs. 5). Third, these four periods are represented in these verses as a temporal development or *progression* involving, in order, pre-creation, creation, incarnation, and the present.[36] Now this is, in fact, the substance and language of the narrow salvation-historical perspective. With no reference to these verses Cullmann himself expresses in italics the essence of this perspective:

---

[35] Cullmann, *Christus und die Zeit*, p. 20. Our discussion has understandably focused on Cullmann, although others too have seen some sort of salvation-history in the Johannine Prologue. Cf. Brown, "The Prologue is a description of the history of salvation in hymnic form. . . ." (*The Gospel according to John*, I, p. 23), and Jeremias who represents the lines of the Prologue as "Heilsgeschichte in Hymnenform" ("The Revealing Word", p. 76).

[36] That these salvation-historical moments culminate with the present is, of course, compatible with realized eschatology, a characteristic emphasis of the Johannine perspective. We do not deny the futuristic features of the Johannine eschatology either in the Gospel or First Epistle, but even in the First Epistle where these are strongest, one feels the force of a statement such as 2:8b (cf. John 1:5).

. . . die verschiedenen Epochen aufeinander folgen, anderseits aber alle [sind] unter sich durch die Orientierung an der sinngebenden Christusmitte verbunden und in ihr zusammengefasst.[37]

We find, then, that approached from a purely textual and exegetical standpoint, John 1:1-5 turns out to be one of those "self-consciously" salvation-historical texts we spoke of earlier. As such it holds new and dramatic implications. First, as concerns the Fourth Gospel, not only can salvation-history not be excluded from this document, but the fact is that this perspective is constitutive of what we believe to be the final and summarizing word of the Johannine School, the Logos hymn.[38] This, taken together with other salvation-historical elements in the Fourth Gospel,[39] suggests that the perspective must be reckoned with as a most salient feature of John's thought. This is not, of course, to exclude from the Johannine theology still other features, but they must at least be compatible with this one. Second, as concerns salvation-history as a general theological position, John 1:1-5 now obviously emerges as a Biblical witness to this position and must be taken along with other such passages as providing together a Biblical foundation for this general theological perspective. All in all, with the salvation-historical interpretation of John 1:1-5—which is, after all, one of the most celebrated passages in the entire Bible, "worthy to be written in gold"—the theology of salvation-history receives not only additional but striking support.

History and Meaning

In the foregoing we have sought to show that John 1:1-5 involves a salvation-historical perspective (and, likely, a salvation-historical hymn), that this perspective coheres with the thought of the Fourth Gospel as a whole, and that the passage must be accepted as further Biblical evidence for the theology of salvation-history. It may be useful, as a final comment, to relate these conclusions to a yet broader theological context.

---

[37] Cullmann, *Heil als Geschichte*, p. 261. It is worth noting, incidentally, that the successive Christological stages are especially emphasized in John inasmuch as only in John, as Brown observes, is the Word called God in his pre-existence (1:1c; even if an interpolation, this line nonetheless represents a genuine Johannine claim), his incarnation (1:18), and his resurrection (20:28) (*The Community of the Beloved Disciple* (New York: Paulist Press, 1979), p. 46).

[38] It will be recalled from the Introduction that we believe that the Logos hymn in John 1:1-5 was the last of the Johannine compositions and was, along with some other Johannine materials, eventually affixed to the Fourth Gospel as a kind of liturgical introduction.

[39] For example, the salvation-historical features that Cullmann finds, mentioned already.

We proceed straight to a *crux* in contemporary theology, namely, to what we might call the problem of history and meaning, or the problem of faith and history. In any case, it is the problem of the relationship between Christian *meaning*, both in the cognitive and existential sense, to *history*, in the sense of factual events. That issue is as complex and difficult as it is fundamental for all theological discussions, and though we refer the reader elsewhere for a complete survey and treatment,[40] the salvation-historical perspective which we have been concerned with throughout forces it to the surface, at least for a moment's consideration.

We therefore record our own agreement with the salvation-historical view, certainly in the wide sense, and, moreover, while we do not subscribe in detail to Cullmann's narrower view of salvation-history, we do believe that it is correct in its fundamental perception that *"alle christliche Theologie ihrem innersten Wesen nach biblische Geschichte ist,"*[41] and we agree with much of the way in which he develops this. At the very least, we believe that the vividly historical character of the Biblical proclamation is the necessary point of departure and a determining feature of any responsible Christian theology. In the same breath, we record also our rejection of any approach which excludes or minimizes the historical-empirical as an essential component of Christian soteriology, or, to distinguish in a manner familiar since Kähler published *Der sogenannte historische Jesus und der geschichtliche, biblische Christus,*[42] any approach which radically divorces the Biblical *Historie*, or straightforward empirical events,[43] from the Biblical *Geschichte*, or the story, meaning, or significance. This insistence on the coherence of *Historie* and *Geschichte*, and even more strongly, the insistence that there can be no authentic meaning, faith, or theology apart from historical-empirical happenings, is, from a strictly theological standpoint, one of the most important features of any salvation-historical perspective. The evidence for all of this is, of course, Biblical (again, Cullmann has no doubt done more than

---

[40] See especially Van Austin Harvey, *The Historian and the Believer: The Morality of Historical Knowledge and Christian Belief* (New York: Macmillan, 1966). One should note also the essays in Carl E. Braaten and Roy A. Harrisville (eds.), *The Historical Jesus and the Kerygmatic Christ* (New York: Abingdon Press, 1964), Leander Keck, *A Future for the Historical Jesus: The Place of Jesus in Preaching and Theology* (Nashville, Tenn.: Abingdon Press, 1971) esp. Ch. 2, and Gordon E. Michaelson, Jr., *Lessing's "Ugly Ditch": A Study of Theology and History* (University Park, Pa.: Pennsylvania State University Press, 1985).

[41] Cullmann, *Christus und die Zeit*, p. 19.

[42] Martin Kähler, *Der sogenannte historische Jesus und der geschichtliche, biblische Christus*, second ed. (Leipzig: Deichert, 1896). This is not to say that Kähler himself would always approve the use to which his distinction has been put.

[43] With most others who treat these matters we believe that there are no "pure" (uninterpreted or intellectually unrelated) empirical facts; nonetheless, with this qualification the above distinction holds and is useful in the present context.

anyone else in amassing this evidence), though it is also theological and even philosophical.

We have in mind, if we may say so, the ultimate vacuity, both cognitively and existentially, of those theologies for which the real significance of the Christ-event is independent of history. Shades and shadows of this *Geschichte*-over-*Historie* approach are discernible everywhere in contemporary theology, but most especially in existentialist strains such as that of Bultmann and Tillich.[44] It is important to note that here it is not just a matter of practical or technical inability to recover knowledge of at least the empirical or outward features of salvation events. If that were so we would be dealing with theologies which would have to grant at least the *theoretical* investigability of such events and, therefore, would have to heed the efforts of those of Bultmann's own disciples who have inaugurated the "new quest" for the historical Jesus.[45]

The claim we are here confronting is a much stronger one. It is the claim that historical investigation is utterly irrelevant inasmuch as the salvation-meaning of the myths, symbols, stories, or whatever, is from the outset and by its very nature entirely independent of any historical, empirical reality. But surely such a self-insulation of Christian meaning, faith, and theology from the objective and common touchstone of historical and empirical happenings sounds the death-knell for genuine, Christian theological truth-claims as well as for the existential appropriation of those claims. Certainly we do not accept an empirical criterion of meaning (an epistemological doctrine that must be repudiated on epistemological grounds), but neither do we know on what basis the truth or falsity of specifically Christian theological claims may be asserted apart from the historical events and contexts to which they trace themselves.[46] On the existential side, apart from an appeal to a theoretically if not actually verifiable/falsifiable foundation, what is the ground and justifica-

---

[44] Rudolf Bultmann, "Neues Testament und Mythologie," in *Kerygma und Mythos*, I, ed. Hans Werner Bartsch (Volksdorf-Hamburg: Evangelischer Verlag, 1948), pp. 44ff. This point of view emerges virtually everywhere in Bultmann's writings, though most notably in the essay just cited and in the little volume, *Jesus Christ and Mythology* (New York: Scribners, 1958); Paul Tillich, *Systematic Theology* (Chicago: University of Chicago Press, 1951-63), II, p. 133ff. It is in Chapter 2 of this volume that Tillich provides his most concentrated treatment of this issue.

[45] See especially Ernst Käsemann's programmatic essay, "Sackgassen im Streit um den historischen Jesus," in *Exegetische Versuche und Besinnungen* (Göttingen: Vandenhoeck & Ruprecht, 1960-64), II, pp. 31ff., and James M. Robinson, *A New Quest of the Historical Jesus* (London: SCM Press, 1959).

[46] Thus one must guardedly take into account the recent and continuing treatments of religious discourse, largely inaugurated by Anthony Flew *et al.* in "Theology and Falsification," in *New Essays in Philosophical Theology*, ed. Anthony Flew and Alasdair MacIntyre (London: SCM Press, 1955), pp. 96ff.

tion of appropriation and its *risk*—unless it be the risk of an utterly subjective or arbitrary decision? A meaning, faith, or theology which cannot
be mistaken is hardly a meaningful one, either cognitively or existentially.[47]

It is easier to be critical than constructive, and we are not indifferent
to the considerations which have led to the *Geschichte*-over-*Historie*
approach, however incoherent it turns out to be. Neither can the
salvation-historical approach, with its conception of *Geschichte*-dependent-
upon-*Historie*, afford to be cavalier on this issue. Therefore, and cutting
straight through the discussions and often conflicting contributions of
many thinkers, such as Lessing, Kierkegaard, Kähler, Troeltsch, Barth,
Brunner, Bultmann, Tillich, Ebeling, Käsemann, Fuchs, and James
Robinson, to mention just a few, we offer a three-sided outline of the
points we see as following necessarily for the problem of faith and history
from any salvation-historical position.

(i) *The theological-Biblical side.* We reiterate that the substance, or at least
an essential feature, of Biblical theology is *Heilsgeschichte* or salvation-
history. We do not insist here on salvation-history in the narrow sense,
as involving, say, a succession of saving events related to one another by
continuity and progression and having at its center the Christ-event and
looking towards the future for its completion. For the following observations it would suffice to affirm a wider conception of salvation-history,
one that insists on history (*Historie*) as the, or at least one, fundamental
category of Biblical and thus Christian theology. God's saving acts
involve, therefore, historical-empirical claims. Here we leave aside the
question of their truth or falsity and insist only on the empirical content
of the claims that to some degree constitute the entire Biblical story and
specifically the story of Jesus Christ. We have to think only of the resurrection of Jesus as involving, at least, the claim, "Jesus was raised from
the dead. . . ." Apart from such a claim (whether true or false), the resurrection would seem to be an unintelligible idea. But God's saving acts are
not exhausted in historical-empirical categories; they involve also
theological meaning, as in the *entire* claim, "Jesus was raised from the
dead by the power of God for our salvation."

(ii) *The historical-philosophical side.* The object of Christian belief is,
therefore, in some respects inseparable from the historical, empirical, etc.
This proposition advances on the earlier ones by emphasizing that what
is *believed* is in some way a historical claim and therefore Christian
theology too is in some way committed to taking such claims seriously.

---

[47] Cf. my brief comments in *God and Reason: A Historical Approach to Philosophical Theology*
(New York: Macmillan, 1972), pp. 219ff.

Because of this, Christian belief and theology have in some respects an objective, factual basis which is in principle, if not in practice, investigable, the object of historical research, verifiable/falsifiable. Thus in some respects Christian belief and theology must be at least in theory conditioned by historical evidence, and in practice open to and vulnerable to the possible findings of historical research. Such evidence can by its nature only be tentative and probable, never conclusive.

(iii) *The practical-existential side.* Historical evidence can never account for the certitude of faith (used here in contrast with belief) with its personal involvement in its object. On the other hand, (passionate) faith presupposes (intellectual) belief and is therefore indirectly conditioned by historical knowledge, and thus involves an objective gamble. It is a constant temptation to confuse faith with belief and thereby to empty Christian faith of its existential content.

To be sure, the historical-empirical content of Christian meaning, faith, and theology must finally be put into perspective. Even if we should accept that such claims are in some way foundational to or presupposed by all the rest, we would have to acknowledge the presence also of many other "languages," as we might call them. It is not just historical or empirical language, but also liturgical, devotional, hortatory, sacramental, allegorical, metaphorical, and apocalyptic languages—each with its own peculiar significance and appropriate mode of validation—that constitute the total Biblical *mythos*. Naturally, one is free, and even impelled, to interpret the Biblical *mythos* for differing times and situations. Nonetheless, if, in the interpretation and resulting theology, history (*Historie*) is excluded as a fundamental and determining category, then that interpretation and theology must be rejected as having substituted some other self-understanding for the Biblical self-understanding.

CONCLUSION

J. A. T. Robinson observed that

> the effect of reading too much on the Fourth Gospel is to make one feel either that everything has been said about it that could conceivably be said or that it really does not matter what one says, for one is just as likely to be right as anyone else.[1]

Certainly the sentiment could *a fortiori* be expressed about the Prologue to the Fourth Gospel, and, as was suggested in the Introduction, many will be naturally skeptical that any radically new theses about the Prologue could be sustained. Nonetheless, that is what has been attempted here.

We have moved from the particular to the general and from the exegetical to the theological. More specifically, we have tried to show that from an analysis of a single problem of punctuation important evidence may be adduced for ὃ γέγονεν as the beginning of John 1:4 (rather than as the conclusion of 1:3), and the theological perspective that this bears on is a salvation-historical one. We review now our central conclusions.

It can be believed on independent grounds that John 1:1-5 contains hymnic materials and probably a complete Christological hymn. This conclusion is, we believe, enhanced by a reconsideration and new interpretation of the always problematic phrase ὃ γέγονεν at 1:3/4. Textual criticism shows, with almost as much certainty as one might hope for, that ὃ γέγονεν properly introduces vs. 4 rather than concludes vs. 3. But this reading of the text, the *lectio difficilior*, poses a most vexing problem for the interpreter. The usual attempts to make good and Johannine sense of this reading founder in one way or another, and we are driven to a radically different interpretation of ὃ γέγονεν ἐν αὐτῷ ζωὴ ἦν, namely, the "incarnational" interpretation. On this view ὃ γέγονεν ἐν αὐτῷ ζωὴ ἦν is a reference to the advent of the Logos into worldly history: "What has appeared in him was life."

The incarnational interpretation of the text is not only compatible with John 1:1-5 conceived as hymnic material, but unlocks the inner logic of these verses. If we delete, as we have argued for but not insisted on, vss. 1c and 2 as interpolations, what remains in 1:1a-b, 3-5 is, we propose, a complete Christological hymn, extolling in four strophes four moments in the unfolding saving activity of the Logos:

---

[1] Robinson, "The Relation of the Prologue to the Gospel of St. John," p. 120.

I. In the beginning was the Logos,
   And the Logos was with God.

II. All things came into being through him,
    And apart from him nothing came into being.

III. What has appeared in him was Life,
     And the Life was the Light of men.

IV. And the Light shines in the Darkness,
    And the Darkness cannot overcome it.

Even if our case for a Christological hymn in these lines fails, our more important thesis about the salvation-historical perspective in these lines is, it seems to us, unassailable. The movement, signalled by four different verb tenses, is from the Logos in his pre-existent relation to God before creation, to the Logos in his creative relation to the world at the time of creation, to the Logos in his salvation-imparting relation to men at the time of incarnation, to the Logos in his victorious relation to evil in the present. This Logos hymn may appropriately be called a salvation-history hymn not only because of its central reference to the historical advent of the Logos—the incarnation—in the third strophe, but, more strikingly, because of the way in which it recounts four successive events or stages in the activity of the Logos as this progressive activity bears on the salvation of men.

The Prologue of John is studded throughout with salvation-historical significance. But the Logos hymn, or at least the lines in 1:1-5, is a sustained salvation-historical representation of the Logos' saving activity, and these verses, among the most celebrated in the Bible, must be taken as further Biblical foundation for the theology of salvation-history.

BIBLIOGRAPHY

Traditional Works

Adamantius, *De Recta in Deum Fide.*
Alexander of Alexandria, *Epistolae.*
Ambrose, *De Fide.*
——, *In Psalmum.*
Augustine, *De Civitate Dei.*
——, *De Trinitate.*
——, *In Ioannis Evangelium.*
Calvin, John, *In Ioannis Evangelium.*
Clement of Alexandria, *Excerpta ex Scriptis Theodoti.*
Cyprian, *Ad Quirinum.*
Didymus, *De Trinitate.*
Epiphanius, *Adversus Octoginta Haereses.*
Erasmus, *Annotationes in Novum Testamentum.*
Eusebius, *De Laudibus Constantini.*
——, *Historia Ecclesiastica.*
——, *Praeparatio Evangelica.*
Heracleon, *In Ioannis Evangelium.*
[Hermes Trismegistos], *Corpus Hermeticum.*
Hilary, *De Trinitate*
Irenaeus, *Adversus Haereses.*
Origen, *In Ioannis Evangelium.*
Philo, *De Opificio Mundi.*
Pliny, *Epistolae.*
Tertullian, *Adversus Hermogenem.*
——, *Adversus Marcionem.*
——, *Adversus Praxeam.*
——, *De Resurrectione Mortuorum.*
Theodoret, *Historia Ecclesiastica.*
Thomas Aquinas, *Lectura super Johannem.*

Modern Works

Aland, Kurt, "Eine Untersuchung zu Joh. 1:3-4: Über die Bedeutung eines Punktes," *ZNW*, 59 (1968), pp. 174ff.
——,*Neutestamentliche Entwürfe* (Munich: Kaiser, 1979).
Atal, Dosithée, *Structure et Signification des Cinq Premiers Versets de L'Hymne Johannique au Logos* (Louvain: Nauwelaerts, 1972).
Barrett, C. K., *The Gospel according to St. John*, second ed. (Philadelphia: Westminster Press, 1978).
——, "Papyrus Bodmer II: A Preliminary Report," *ET*, 68 (1956-57), pp. 174ff..
——, "The Prologue of St. John's Gospel," in *New Testament Essays* (London: SPCK, 1972), pp. 27ff.
Barth, Karl, *Erklärung des Johannes-Evangeliums (Kapitel 1-8)*, ed. Walther Fürst, (Zurich: Theologischer Verlag, 1976).
Bauer, Walter, *A Greek-English Lexicon of the New Testament and Other Early Christian Literature*, tr. William F. Arndt and F. Wilbur Gingrich, second ed., ed. F. Wilbur Gingrich and Frederick W. Danker (Chicago: University of Chicago Press, 1979).

——, *Das Johannesevangelium*, second ed. (Tübingen: Mohr, 1925).

Bernard, J. H., *A Critical and Exegetical Commentary on the Gospel according to St. John*, ed. A. H. McNeile (Edinburgh: Clark, 1928), 2 vols.

Black, Matthew, *An Aramaic Approach to the Gospels and Acts*, third ed. (Oxford, England: Clarendon Press, 1967).

Blass, F., and Debrunner, A., *A Greek Grammar of the New Testament and Other Early Christian Literature*, tr. and rev. Robert W. Funk (Chicago: University of Chicago Press, 1961).

Boismard, M.-E., *Le Prologue de Saint Jean*, (Paris: Les Editions du Cerf, 1953).

Borgen, Peder, "Logos was the True Light: Contributions to the Interpretation of the Prologue of John," *NT*, 14 (1972), pp. 115ff.

——, "Observations on the Targumic Character of the Prologue of John," *NTS*, 16 (1970), pp. 288ff.

Braaten, Carl E., and Harrisville, Roy A. (eds.), *The Historical Jesus and the Kerygmatic Christ* (New York: Abingdon, 1964).

Braun, F.-M., "L'Arrière-fond Judaïque du Quatrième Évangile et la Communauté de l'Alliance," *RB*, 62 (1955), pp. 5ff.

Brown, Raymond E., *The Community of the Beloved Disciple* (New York: Paulist Press, 1979).

——, *The Epistles of John* (Garden City, N. Y.: Doubleday, 1982).

——, *The Gospel according to John* (Garden City, N. Y.: Doubleday, 1966-70), 2 vols.

Bultmann, Rudolf, "Die Eschatologie des Johannes-Evangeliums," *Glauben und Verstehen*: *Gesammelte Aufsätze*, I (Tübingen: Mohr, 1933), pp. 134ff.

——, *Das Evangelium des Johannes* (Göttingen: Vandenhoeck & Ruprecht, 1941).

——, "Heilsgeschichte und Geschichte: Zu O. Cullmann, Christus und die Zeit," *TL*, 73 (1948), pp. 659ff.

——, *Jesus Christ and Mythology* (New York: Scribners, 1958).

——, "Neues Testament und Mythologie," *Kerygma und Mythos*, ed. Hans Werner Bartsch (Volksdorf-Hamburg: Evangelischer Verlag, 1948), pp. 15ff.

——, "Der religionsgeschichtliche Hintergrund des Prologs zum Johannes-Evangelium," in *EYXAPIΣTHPION: Studien zur Religion und Literatur des Alten und Neuen Testaments*, ed. Hans Schmidt (Göttingen: Vandenhoeck & Ruprecht, 1923), II, pp. 3ff.

——, "Ζωή (E.6)," in *TWNT*, II, pp. 871ff.

Buri, Fritz, "Das Problem der ausgebliebenen Parusie," *STU*, 16 (1946), pp. 97ff.

Burney, Charles Fox, *The Aramaic Origin of the Fourth Gospel* (Oxford, England: Oxford University Press, 1922).

Carroll, William, "St. Augustine on John 1:1-5" (unpublished).

Clark, Kenneth, "The Text of the Gospel of John in Third-Century Egypt," *NT*, 5 (1962), pp. 17ff.

Coetzee, J. C., "Life (Eternal Life) in John's Writings and the Qumran Scrolls," *Neotestamentica*, 6 (1972), pp. 48ff.

Colwell, Ernest C., "Methods in Evaluating Scribal Habits: A Study of P^{45}, P^{66}, P^{75}," in *Studies in Methodology in Textual Criticism of the New Testament* (Grand Rapids, Mich.: Eerdmans, 1969), pp. 106ff.

Conzelmann, Hans, "Φῶς (E. IV.1)," in *TWNT*, IX, pp. 341ff.

Corell, Alf, *Consummatum Est: Eskatologi och Kyrka i Johannesevangeliet* (Stockholm: Svenska Kyrkans Diakonistyrelses Bokförlag, 1950).

Cribbs, F. Lamar, "A Reassessment of the Date of Origin and Destination of the Gospel of John," *JBL*, 89 (1970), pp. 38ff.

Cullmann, Oscar, *Die Christologie des Neuen Testaments*, fourth ed. (Tübingen: Mohr, 1966).

——, *Christus und die Zeit: Die urchristliche Zeit- und Geschichtsauffassung* (Zollikon-Zurich: Evangelischer Verlag, 1946).

——, "L'Évangile Johannique et l'Histoire du Salut." *NTS*, 11 (1964-65), pp. 111ff.

——, "Foundations: The Theology of Salvation History and the Ecumenical Dialogue," in *Vatican II: The New Direction*, ed. James D. Hester, tr. James D. Hester *et al*. (New York: Harper & Row, 1968), p 33ff.

——, *Heil als Geschichte: Heilsgeschichtliche Existenz im Neuen Testament* (Tübingen: Mohr, 1965).

——, *Der johanneische Kreis: Sein Platz im Spätjudentum, in der Jüngerschaft Jesu und im Urchristentum* (Tübingen: Mohr, 1975).

——, "Zur Diskussion des Problems der ausgebliebenen Parusie: Replik," *TZ*, 3 (1947), pp. 422ff.

Culpepper, R. Alan, "The Pivot of John's Prologue," *NTS*, 27 (1979), pp. 1ff.

Daniels, Boyd L. and Suggs, M. Jack (eds.), *Studies in the History and Text of the New Testament* (Salt Lake City: University of Utah Press, 1967).

De Ausejo, Serafín, "¿Es un Himno a Cristo el Prólogo de San Juan? Los Himnos Cristologicos de la Iglesia Primitiva y el Prólogo del IV Evangelio," *EB*, 15 (1956), pp. 223ff, 381ff.

De la Potterie, I., "De Interpunctione et Interpretatione Versuum Joh. 1:3-4," *VD*, 33 (1955), pp. 193ff.

——, "De Punctuatie en de Exegese van Joh. 1:3-4 in de Traditie," *Bijdragen*, 16 (1955), pp. 117ff.

——, "Een nieuwe papyrus van het vierde Evangilie, Papyrus Bodmer II," *Bijdragen*, 18 (1957).

——, "Structure du Prologue de Saint Jean," *NTS*, 30 (1984), pp. 354ff.

——, *La Vérité dans St. Jean* (Rome: Biblical Institute Press, 1977), 2 vols.

Deichgräber, Reinhard, *Gotteshymnus und Christushymnus in der frühen Christenheit: Untersuchungen zu Form, Sprache und Stil der frühchristlichen Hymnen* (Göttingen: Vandenhoeck & Ruprecht, 1967).

Demke, Christoph, "Der sogenannte Logos-Hymnus im johanneischen Prolog," *ZNW*, 58 (1967), pp. 45ff.

Dodd, C. H., *Historical Tradition in the Fourth Gospel* (Cambridge, England: Cambridge University Press, 1965).

——, *The Interpretation of the Fourth Gospel* (Cambridge, England: Cambridge University Press, 1953).

——, "The Prologue to the Fourth Gospel and Christian Worship," in *Studies in the Fourth Gospel*, ed. F. L. Cross (London: Mowbray, 1957), pp. 9ff.

Eltester, Walther, "Der Logos und sein Prophet: Fragen zur heutigen Erklärung des johanneischen Prologs," in *Apophoreta* (Berlin: Töpelmann, 1964), pp. 109ff.

Epp, Eldon J., "Wisdom, Torah, Word: The Johannine Prologue and the Purpose of the Fourth Gospel," in *Current Issues in Biblical and Patristic Interpretation*, ed. Gerald F. Hawthorne (Grand Rapids, Mich.: Eerdmans, 1975), pp. 128ff.

Feuillet, A., *Le Prologue du Quatrième Évangile: Étude de Théologie Johannique* (Paris: Desclée de Brouwer, 1968).

Filson, Floyd V., "The Gospel of Life: A Study in the Gospel of John," in *Current Issues in New Testament Interpretation*, ed. William Klassen and Graydon F. Snyder (New York: Harper & Row, 1962), pp. 111ff.

Flew, Antony, Hare, R. M., and Mitchell, Basil, "Theology and Falsification," in *New Essays in Philosophical Theology*, ed. Antony Flew and Alasdair MacIntyre (London: SCM Press, 1955), pp. 96ff.

Freed, Edwin D., "Some Old Testament Influences on the Prologue of John," in *A Light unto My Path: Old Testament Studies in Honor of Jacob M. Myers*, ed. Howard N. Bream, Ralph D. Heim, Carey A. Moore (Philadelphia: Temple University Press, 1974), pp. 145ff.

Frisque, Jean, *Oscar Cullmann: Une Theologie de l'Histoire du Salut* (Tournai: Casterman, 1960).

Fröhlich, Karlfried, "Die Mitte des Neuen Testaments: Oscar Cullmanns Beiträge zur Theologie des Gegenwart," in *Oikonomia: Heilsgeschichte als Thema der Theologie*, ed. Felix Christ (Hamburg: Reich, 1967), pp. 203ff.

Gächter, Paul, "Strophen im Johannesevangelium," *ZKT*, 60 (1936), pp. 99ff.

Gennaro, Julianus, *Exegetica in Prologum sec. Maximos Ecclesiae Doctores Antiquitatis Christianae* (Rome: Pontificium Athenaeum Antonianum, 1952).

Gese, Hartmut, "Der Johannesprolog," in *Zur biblischen Theologie: Altestamentliche Vorträge* (Munich: Kaiser, 1977), pp. 152ff.

Giblin, Charles Homer, "Two Complementary Literary Structures in John 1:1-18," *JBL*, 104 (1985), pp. 87ff.

Goppelt, Leonhard, *Theologie des Neuen Testaments* (Göttingen: Vandenhoeck & Ruprecht, 1975-76), 2 vols.

Green, Humphrey C., "The Composition of St. John's Prologue," *ET*, 66 (1954-55), pp. 291ff.

Haacker, Klaus, "Eine formgeschichtliche Beobachtung zu Joh. 1:3 fin.," *BZ*, 12 (1968), pp. 119ff.

Haenchen, Ernst, *A Commentary on the Gospel of John*, ed. Ulrich Busse, tr. and ed. Robert W. Funk (Philadelphia: Fortress Press, 1984).

——, *Das Johannesevangelium*, ed. Ulrich Busse (Tübingen: Mohr, 1980).

——, "Probleme des johanneischen 'Prologs,'" *ZTK*, 60 (1963)

Hammerton-Kelly, R. G., *Pre-existence Wisdom and the Son of Man: A Study of the Idea of Pre-existence in the New Testament* (Cambridge, England: Cambridge University Press, 1973).

Harvey, Van Austin, *The Historian and the Believer: The Morality of Historical Knowledge and Christian Belief* (New York: Macmillan, 1966).

Hermesmann, Hans-Georg, *Zeit und Heil: Oscar Cullmanns Theologie der Heilsgeschichte* (Paderborn: Bonifacius, 1979).

Hesse, Franz, *Abschied von der Heilsgeschichte* (Zurich: Theologischer Verlag, 1971).

Hirsch, Emanuel, *Studien zum vierten Evangelium* (Tübingen: Mohr, 1936).

Hofrichter, Peter, " 'Egeneto anthropos': Text und Zusätze im Johannesprolog," *ZNW*, 70 (1979), pp. 214ff.

Hooker, Morna, "John the Baptist and the Johannine Prologue," *NTS*, 16 (1970), pp. 354ff.

——, "The Johannine Prologue and the Messianic Secret," *NTS*, 21 (1975), pp. 40ff.

Hoskyns, Edwyn Clement, *The Fourth Gospel*, ed. Francis Noel Davey, second ed. (London: Faber, 1947).

Howard, Wilbert F. in *The Interpreter's Bible*, VIII (with Arthur John Gossip), *The Gospel according to St. John* (New York: Abingdon Press, 1952).

Hunger, Herbert, "Zur Datierung des Papyrus Bodmer II (P^{66})," *Anzeiger der öster-reichischen Akademie der Wissenschaften*, phil.-hist. Kl., 4 (1966), pp. 12ff.

Ibuki, Yu, "Offene Fragen zur Aufnahme des Logoshymnus in das vierte Evangelium," *Annual of the Japanese Biblical Institute*, 5 (1979), pp. 105ff.

Irigoin, Jean, "La Composition rhythmique du Prologue de Jean (1:1-18)," *RB*, 72 (1971), pp. 501ff.

Jeremias, Joachim, "The Revealing Word," in *The Central Message of the New Testament* (Philadelphia: Fortress Press, 1965), pp. 71ff.

Kähler, Martin, *Der sogennante historische Jesus und der geschichtliche, biblische Christus*, second ed. (Leipzig: Deichert, 1896).

Käsemann, Ernst, "Aufbau und Anliegen des johanneischen Prologs," in *Libertas Christiana* (Munich: Kaiser, 1957), pp. 75ff.

——, *Jesu letzter Wille nach Johannes 17* (Tübingen: Mohr 1966).

——, "Rechtfertigung und Heilsgeschichte im Römerbrief," in *Paulinische Perspektiven* (Tübingen: Mohr, 1969), pp. 108ff.

——, "Sackgassen im Streit um den historischen Jesus," *Exegetische Versuche und Besinnungen* (Göttingen: Vandenhoeck & Ruprecht, 1964), II, pp. 31ff.

Keck, Leander, *A Future for the Historical Jesus: The Place of Jesus in Preaching and Theology* (Nashville, Tenn.: Abingdon Press, 1971).

Kemper, Friedmar, "Zur literarischen Gestalt des Johannesevangeliums," *TZ*, 43 (1987), pp. 247ff.

King, J. S. "The Prologue to the Fourth Gospel: Some Unsolved Problems," *ET*, 86 (1974), pp. 372ff.

Klein, Günter, "Bibel und Heilsgeschichte," *ZNW*, 62 (1971), pp. 1ff.

Kümmel, W. G., "Heilsgeschichte im Neuen Testament," in *Neues Testament und Kirche*, ed. J. Gnilka (Freiburg/Breisgau: Herder, 1974), pp. 31ff.

114   BIBLIOGRAPHY

Kysar, Robert, "The Background of the Prologue of the Fourth Gospel," *CJT*, 16 (1970), pp. 250ff.

——, "R. Bultmann's Interpretation of the Concept of Creation in John 1:3-4: A Study of Exegetical Method," *CBQ*, 32 (1970), pp. 77ff.

Lacan, M.-F., "L'Oeuvre du Verbe Incarné: Le Don de la Vie," *RSR*, 45 (1957), pp. 61ff.

Lagrange, M.-J., *Évangile selon Saint Jean*, third ed. (Paris: Gabalda, 1927).

Lamarche, P., "Le Prologue de Jean," *RSR*, 52 (1964), pp. 497ff.

Lightfoot, R. H., *St. John's Gospel: A Commentary with the Revised Version Text*, ed. C. F. Evans (Oxford, England: Oxford University Press, 1956).

Lindars, Barnabas, *The Gospel of John* (London: Oliphants, 1972).

Loisy, Alfred, *Le Quatrième Évangile*, second ed. (Paris: Nourry, 1921; first ed., Paris: Picard, 1903).

Löwith, Karl, *Meaning in History: The Theological Implications of the Philosophy of History* (Chicago: University of Chicago Press, 1949).

MacGregor, G. H. C., *The Gospel of John* (Garden City, N. Y.: Doubleday, 1929).

Malatesta, Edward, *St. John's Gospel 1920-1965: A Cumulative and Classified Bibliography of Books and Periodical Literature on the Fourth Gospel* (Rome: Pontifical Biblical Institute, 1967).

Marsh, John, *The Gospel of St. John* (Baltimore, Md.: Penguin Books, 1968).

Martin, R. P., *Carmen Christi: Philippians ii. 5-11 in Recent Interpretation and in the Setting of Early Christian Worship* (Cambridge, England: Cambridge University Press, 1967).

Martin, Victor and Kasser, Rodolphe (eds.), *Papyrus Bodmer XIV-XV: Évangile de Luc, chap. 3-24, Évangile de Jean, chap. 1-15* (Cologny-Geneva: Bibliotheca Bodmeriana, 1961), 2 vols.

Martin, Victor (ed.), *Papyrus Bodmer II: Évangile de Jean, chap. 1-14* (Cologny-Geneva: Bibliotheca Bodmeriana, 1958), revised ed. Victor Martin and J. W. B. Barns (1962).

Massaux, Édouard, "Le Papyrus Bodmer II (P⁶⁶) et la Critique Néo-testamentaire," in *Sacra Pagina: Miscellanea Biblica Congressus Internationalis Catholici de re Biblica*, ed. J. Coppens, A. Descamps, and É. Massaux (Gembloux: J. Duculot, 1959), I, pp. 194ff.

Mateos, Juan, and Barreto, Juan, *El Evangelio de Juan: Analisis Linguistico y Commentario Exegetico* (Madrid: Ediciones Cristiandad, 1979).

Mehlmann, John, "A Note on John 1:3," *ET*, 67 (1955-56), pp. 340f.

Metzger, Bruce M., "The Bodmer Papyrus of Luke and John," *ET*, 73 (1961-62), pp. 201ff.

——, *Historical and Literary Studies* (Leiden: Brill, 1968).

——, "The Language of the New Testament," in *The Interpreter's Bible* (New York: Abingdon Press, 1951), VII, pp. 43ff.

——, "Patristic Evidence and the Textual Criticism of the New Testament," *NTS*, 18 (1971-72), pp. 379ff.

——, *A Textual Commentary on the Greek New Testament* (London: United Bible Societies, 1971).

Michalson, Gordon E., Jr., *Lessing's "Ugly Ditch": A Study of Theology and History* (University Park, Pa.: Pennsylvania State University Press, 1985).

Miller, Ed. L., "Codex Bezae on John 1:3-4: One Dot or Two?," *TZ*, 32 (1976), pp. 269ff.

——, *God and Reason: A Historical Approach to Philosophical Theology* (New York: Macmillan, 1972).

——, "The Logic of the Logos Hymn: A New View," *NTS*, 29 (1983), pp. 552ff.

——, "The *Logos* was God," *EQ*, 53 (1981), pp. 65ff.

——, "P⁶⁶ and P⁷⁵ on John 1:3/4," *TZ*, 41 (1985), pp. 440ff.

Morris, Leon, *The Gospel according to John* (Grand Rapids, Mich.: Eerdmans, 1971).

Müller-Fahrenholz, Geiko, *Heilsgeschichte zwischen Ideologie und Prophetie: Profile und Kritik heilsgeschichtlicher Theorien der ökumenischen Bewegung zwischen 1948 und 1968* (Freiburg/Breisgau: Herder, 1974).

Mussner, Franz, *ZΩH: Die Anschauung vom "Leben" im vierten Evangelium unter Berücksichtigung der Johannesbriefe* (Munich: Fink, 1952).

O'Neill, J. C., "The Prologue to St. John's Gospel," *JTS*, 20 (1969), pp. 41ff.

Pagels, Elaine H., *The Johannine Gospel in Gnostic Exegesis: Heracleon's Commentary on John* (Nashville, Tenn.: Abingdon Press, 1973).

Painter, John, "Christology and the History of the Johannine Community in the Prologue of the Fourth Gospel," *NTS*, 30 (1984), pp. 460ff.

Pannenberg, Wolfhart, "Weltgeschichte und Heilsgeschichte," in *Geschichte-Ereignis und Erzählung*, ed. Reinhart Koselleck and Wolf-Dieter Stempel (Munich: Fink, 1973), pp. 307ff.

Pollard, Evan T., "Cosmology and the Prologue of the Fourth Gospel," *VC*, 12 (1958), pp. 147ff.

Porter, Calvin, "Papyrus Bodmer XV (P^{75}) and the Text of Codex Vaticanus," *JBL*, 81 (1962), pp. 363ff.

Prete, Benedetto, "La Concordanza del Participio ἐρχόμενον in Giov. 1:9," *Bibbia et Oriente*, 17 (1975), pp. 195ff.

Richter, Georg, "Ist ἐν ein strukturbildendes Element im Logoshymnus Joh. 1:1ff.?" *Biblica*, 51 (1970), pp. 539ff.

Ridderbos, Hermann, "The Structure and Scope of the Prologue to the Gospel of John," *NT*, 8 (1966), pp. 180ff.

Rissi, Mathias, "Die Logoslieder im Prolog des vierten Evangeliums," *TZ*, 31 (1975), pp. 321ff.

Robertson, A. T., *A Grammar of the Greek New Testament in the Light of Historical Research*, fourth ed. (New York: Hodder & Stoughton, 1923).

Robinson, James M., *A New Quest of the Historical Jesus* (London: SCM Press, 1959).

Robinson, John A. T., *The Priority of John*, ed. J. F. Coakley (London: S. C. M. Press, 1985).

——, *Redating the New Testament* (Philadelphia: Westminster Press, 1976).

——, "The Relation of the Prologue to the Gospel of St. John," *NTS*, 9 (1962-63), pp. 120ff.

Rochais, Gérard, "La Formation du Prologue (Jn. 1:1-18)," *SE*, 37 (1985), pp. 5ff., 161ff.

Ruckstuhl, Eugen, "Kritische Arbeit am Johannesprolog," in *The New Testament Age*, ed. William C. Weinrich (Atlanta: Mercer University Press, 1984), II, pp. 443ff.

——, *Die literarische Einheit des Johannesevangeliums: Der gegenwärtige Stand der einschlägigen Forschungen* (Freiburg/Schweiz: Paulus, 1951).

Sanders, J. N. and Mastin, B. A., *A Commentary on the Gospel according to St. John* (London: Black, 1968).

Sanders, Jack T., *The New Testament Christological Hymns: Their Historical Religious Background* (Cambridge, England: Cambridge University Press, 1971).

Schille, Gottfried, *Frühchristliche Hymnen* (Berlin: Evangelische Verlagsanstalt, 1962).

Schlatter, Adolf, *Der Evangelist Johannes: Wie Er Spricht, Denkt und Glaubt* (Stuttgart: Calwer, 1930).

Schlatter, Frederic W., "The Problem of Jn. 1:3b-4a," *CBQ*, 34 (1972), pp. 54ff.

Schlier, Heinrich, "Im Anfang war das Wort: Zum Prolog des Johannesevangeliums," in *Die Zeit der Kirche: Exegetische Aufsätze und Vorträge* (Freiburg/Breisgau: Herder, 1956), pp. 274ff.

Schmithals, Walter, "Der Prologue des Johannesevangeliums," *ZNW*, 70 (1979), pp. 16ff.

Schnackenburg, Rudolf, *Das Johannesevangelium* (Freiburg/Breisgau: Herder, 1965-75), 3 vols.

——, "Logos-Hymnus und johanneischer Prolog," *BZ*, 1 (1957), pp. 69ff.

Schultz, Siegfried, *Das Evangelium nach Johannes* (Göttingen: Vandenhoeck & Ruprecht, 1972).

——, *Komposition und Herkunft der Johanneischen Reden* (Stuttgart: Kohlhammer, 1960).

Schwartz, Eduard, "Aporien im vierten Evangelium, IV," *Nachrichten von der königlichen Gesellschaft der Wissenschaften zu Göttingen*, phil.-hist. Kl. (1908), pp. 497ff.

Smalley, Stephen S., *John: Evangelist and Interpreter* (Exeter: Paternoster, 1978).

Smyth, Herbert Weir, *Greek Grammar*, rev. Gordon M. Messing (Cambridge, Mass.: Harvard University Press, 1959).

Steck, Karl Gerhard, *Die Idee der Heilsgeschichte: Hofmann–Schlatter–Cullmann* (Zolliken-Zurich: Evangelischer Verlag, 1959).

Teeple, Howard M., *The Literary Origin of the Gospel of John* (Evanston, Ill.: Religion and Ethics Institute, 1974).

——, and Walker, F. A., "Notes on the Plates in Papyrus Bodmer II," *JBL*, 78 (1959), pp. 148ff.

Theobald, Michael, *Im Anfang war das Wort: Textlinguistische Studie zum Johannesprolog* (Stuttgart: Katholisches Bibelwerk, 1983).

Thyen, Hartwig, "Aus der Literatur zum Johannesevangelium, I," *TR*, 39 (1975), pp. 1ff.

Tillich, Paul, *Systematic Theology* (Chicago: University of Chicago Press, 1951-63), 3 vols.

Van den Bussche, H., "Quod Factum Est, in Ipso Vita Erat (Jo. 1:3-4)," *Collationes Brugenses et Gandavensis*, 2 (1956), pp. 85ff.

——, "De tout Être la Parole était la Vie: Jean 1:1-5," *BVC*, 69 (1966) pp. 57ff.

Van Hoonacker, Albin August, "Le Prologue du Quatrième Évangile," *RHE*, 2 (1901).

Vanderlip, D. George, *Christianity according to John* (Philadelphia: Westminster Press, 1975).

Vawter, Bruce, "What Came to Be in Him Was Life (Jn. 1:3b-4a)," *CBQ*, 25 (1963), pp. 401ff..

Weisengoff, J. P., "Light and Its Relation to Life in Saint John," *CBQ*, 8 (1946), pp. 48ff.

Weiss, Bernhard, *Das Evangelium des Johannes: Kritischer und exegetischer Kommentar*, (Göttingen: Vandenhoeck & Ruprecht, 1880).

Westcott, B. F., *The Gospel according to St. John* (Grand Rapids, Mich: Eerdmans, 1978 (orig. 1880)).

Wiles, Maurice F., *The Spiritual Gospel: The Interpretation of the Fourth Gospel in the Early Church* (Cambridge, England: Cambridge University Press, 1960).

Zahn, Theodor, *Das Evangelium des Johannes*, fifth and sixth eds. (Leipzig: Deichert, 1921).

Zerwick, Maximilian, *Biblical Greek*, fourth ed., tr. and rev. Joseph Smith (Rome: Pontifical Biblical Institute, 1963).

Zimmermann, Heinrich, "Christushymnus und johanneischer Prolog," in *Neues Testament und Kirche*, ed. Joachim Gnilka (Freiburg/Breisgau Herder, 1974), pp. 249ff.

INDEX OF NAMES